How to Reach the
Hard to Teach

Open University Press
Children with Special Needs Series

Editors

PHILLIP WILLIAMS
Professor and Head of the School of Education,
University College of North Wales, Bangor.

PETER YOUNG
Formerly Tutor in the education of children with
learning difficulties, Cambridge Institute of Education;
educational writer, researcher and consultant.

Both Phillip Williams and Peter Young were members
of the Warnock Committee of Enquiry into the Education
of Handicapped Children and Young People.

This is a series of short and authoritative introductions for parents, teachers, professionals and anyone concerned with children with special needs. The series will cover the range of physical, sensory, mental, emotional and behavioural difficulties, and the changing needs from infancy to adult life in the family, at school and in society. The authors have been selected for their wide experience and close professional involvement in their particular fields. All have written penetrating and practical books readily accessible to non-specialists.

TITLES IN THE SERIES

How to Reach the
Hard to Teach

Older pupils with special needs

Paul Widlake

Open University Press
Milton Keynes

Open University Press
A division of
Open University Educational Enterprises Limited
12 Cofferidge Close
Stony Stratford
Milton Keynes MK11 1BY, England.

British Library Cataloguing in Publication Data

Widlake, Paul
    How to reach the hard to teach
    1. Education, Secondary – Great Britain – Curricula
    2. Slow learning children – Great Britain
    I. Title
    371.92'6   LB1629.5.G7

    ISBN 0–335–10195–X
    ISBN 0–335–10194–1 Pbk

Text design by W.A.P.

Typeset by Freeman Graphic, Tonbridge
Printed in Great Britain by
St. Edmundsbury Press, Bury St. Edmunds, Suffolk.

Contents

Editors' Introduction

This book adopts a constructive and positive posture in confronting the complex and extensive problem of educating young people with special educational and other needs in our comprehensive schools. Perceptive and incisive in its diagnosis of the social and cultural factors affecting these pupils, what is surprising, refreshing and thoroughly worth while about Paul Widlake's approach is that he identifies so many significant and relevant examples of good practice, experimentation, curriculum development and organization in form-rooms, schools and local educational authorities up and down the country. He doesn't exhort but he does show what can be done and how to do it.

Paul Widlake's book is not about abstract problems which are, of course, susceptible to abstract solutions, but about people. This is an important and vital distinction which he successfully establishes from the outset. He is concerned for real pupils with real problems in a harsh and demanding world. Unless the reader has seen something of that world at first hand it may be difficult to appreciate how it affects pupils and acts as a constraint upon their teachers. It is a part of the author's success that he enables us to see more sensitively and perceptively within that situation. Unemployment, changing family structures, the complexity and tensions of multiracial and multiethnic communities, the conflict between pupils' perception of wealth and power and the poverty of their own opportunities and environments, the demands of new technologies and the constraints of old and inadequate ones, are factors which we ignore in education at our peril. But what we do about them is an even more demanding responsibility. It is one which this book faces squarely. Again, daunting though the

task may be, Paul Widlake presents it as an exciting and rewarding opportunity.

The book articulates this approach by example. Gradually one
becomes aware that all the examples demonstrate that schools
which successfully and progressively meet the needs of the hard
to teach are schools which are themselves concerned to learn.
They are concerned to learn about their pupils, their pupils'
situations, hopes and needs, to learn more about their curricula
and their relevance to their pupils and society, and to learn more
about the communities and the society they serve. They are also
schools which are concerned to make learning and the community of the school enjoyable for pupils and staff alike. Perhaps
it is because these concerns are so manifest in this book that
reading it is a stimulating experience. For not only is so much of
what is described practical and realizable with these pupils;
clearly, too, it is worth while and enjoyable.

It is a mark of the great change which has overtaken education
that only a few years ago it was possible to talk about significant
living without work solely in connection with those people so
badly handicapped that they would not be given a job even in a
sheltered workshop. Now we must take on board that concept for
our most able, too. Although Paul Widlake is neither prescriptive
nor didactic, he is excitingly illuminative and alerts us both to the
changes going on in our schools and to the ways in which these
new opportunities for organic growth and development may be
put to best use in reaching the hard to teach and helping them to
construct themselves and their world. In doing so he has provided a source book of ideas, examples of practical approaches
and designs for learning across the curriculum which should be
read by everyone concerned for the quality of education in our
schools and for the quality of the lives of these young people.

Phillip Williams
Peter Young

Preface

There are few books which deal with older pupils with learning difficulties in ordinary as opposed to special schools in the British state education system. Unlike some critics, I believe that much can be achieved from within this system, despite its many inadequacies and shortcomings and occasional spectacular failures. This belief is based upon observations of many secondary schools which do provide excellent learning opportunities for most of their pupils. There is no doubt that schools can make a great difference: humane, well-organized, community-orientated secondary schools can be exciting places which, through the variety and scope of their educational provision, attract and retain the attention of many pupils who in other schools become dropouts.

It is a rewarding task to review the efforts of strong staffs, well supported by local authorities, but to limit one's observations to such schools would be to provide a distorted picture. Many schools are in desperate straits and in some local authorities educational policies are being pursued which make the tasks of teachers very difficult. However, given proper conditions, teachers are demonstrating all over the country that they can help almost any child, even those with quite severe disabilities, within the ordinary school system.

Schools should be alive with activity, opening their doors to a wide age and ability range, sensitive to community needs yet fully responsive to the special educational needs of individual pupils. All this has to be done, however, at a time when British society is being subjected to changes of a scope and depth which threaten to sweep away familiar landscapes. No wonder teachers, who are in the front line, find it difficult to adjust, or even to know what to adjust to!

In this book there is a strong emphasis upon people. I am suggesting that teachers as well as pupils examine their own behaviour and, if necessary, alter it. Every chapter in the book is concerned with the question: how can schools become better able to meet their pupils' special educational needs? The answer concentrates upon three main points.

First, improvements in the quality of interaction between pupils and teachers; between teachers and teachers; between teachers and parents; between teachers and other professionals or para-professionals; and between school staffs and members of the community. In good schools all these people share a common purpose, a common sense of excitement and achievement. This book calls on teachers (preferably with parental support in some form or other) to be active in decision making; it makes practical suggestions as to how this might be accomplished; it is intended as a text for those who wish to initiate changes through school-based in-service education and self-assessment.

The second point of emphasis is on the assessment and treatment of learning difficulties. Even those schools which have extended their horizons in the ways advocated often fail in dealing with pupils with learning difficulties. Very few teachers are able to turn the "literature" into practicable learning pro-grammes which are robust enough to survive the hurly-burly of a large secondary school. Perhaps this helps to explain the occasional lack of self-confidence on the part of supposedly specialist teachers: the procedures they have so painfully mastered on advanced level courses do not seem to have much relevance to the pupils they are actually called upon to deal with. This is especially obvious as the pupils grow older.

Thirdly, I suggest that this situation can be improved by concentrating attention more upon the conditions which make for effective learning among older pupils and by adapting curriculum materials and ideas to their needs – consulting them whenever possible. There is an enormous amount of material published and ready for use, but it mostly remains an untapped resource. Why should this be the case? How can the curriculum which is offered to the "hard to teach" be made more relevant to their needs and more palatable?

By and large, it seems, secondary schools are too stiff and formal. They are stuck with inadequate curricula, derived from external examinations which have no possible application to the needs of the bottom 20 per cent or so in the schools' "attainment lists". Indeed, the examinations are designed to select and exclude, to allow the intellectual élite to demonstrate their aptitude for higher education. Quite a few schools, however, are already thinking about programmes for an 11 to 21-year-old clientele, thus letting in fresh air from the entirely different and very pragmatic traditions which have been built up by tutors working in colleges of further education and on courses provided under the aegis of the Manpower Services Commission. Others have introduced alternative assessment procedures which emphasize achievements and involve some self-appraisal and, hence, self-involvement. The opportunity exists to create a new pedagogy which, if seized, will enable schools to respond with fresh vigour to special educational needs, free at last from the dead hand of normative testing and its associated labelling, free from circumscribing preconceptions of what constitutes acceptable material for a school's curriculum.

Acknowledgements

This book owes a great deal to my former colleagues and students at Manchester Polytechnic, particularly those who came on the various in-service courses for teachers. This was where most of my thinking about special educational needs was done. Subsequently, at the Community Education Development Centre in Coventry, a community dimension was added. I am grateful for the stimulus these contrasting venues have provided.

I have had maximum support from the Series Editors and the Open University Press.

Thus stimulated and guided, I have to accept sole responsibility for such faults as the book may be found to contain.

CHAPTER 1

Who are the Hard to Teach?

I shall not readily forget the young teacher who stood up to ask me a question after I had given one of my talks on learning difficulties. Barely containing her tears, she asked how she could possibly do justice to a physically disabled pupil who had been added to the 35 eleven-year-olds she was already teaching, many of whom had considerable difficulties in reading and mathematics, or behavioural problems. She was completely willing to undertake the responsibility, but was being offered no additional facilities or resources, without which she could not cope. This is the other side of the coin of integration. It is cruel thus to abuse willing and reasonably successful teachers; it is still more cruel to abuse disabled and failing pupils. It is all the more unacceptable because many secondary schools do receive groups of physically disabled pupils and, given the necessary and sufficient conditions, look after them admirably.

One of many examples is a middle school in Leeds which has incorporated physically disabled pupils as normal class members. They follow the same timetable as other pupils as far as possible. One extra member of staff (designated as PH tutor) arranges special activities: hydrotherapy, for example, in place of physical education. The tutor sees the pupils daily, attends medical sessions and keeps in touch with the parents. Twenty-four disabled pupils have attended the school over a period of six years, with between six and ten pupils at the school at any one time. The disabilities have spanned a wide range, including spina bifida, paralysis and haemophilia. Special facilities at the school are kept to a minimum. They include special toilets, back-up facilities for physiotherapy and hydrotherapy, electric typewriters and ramps for pupils in wheelchairs. When physically disabled

1

pupils leave at 13+, they go to the adjoining single-storey high
school, which has incorporated ramps into its design.[1]

It is extremely encouraging that teachers in both ordinary and
special schools are willing to accept additional responsibilities of
this order.[2] Unfortunately, for a number of reasons, the British
state educational system rarely produces such excellent conditions and quite frequently produces the opposite. Under adverse
conditions, it is not only impossible to look after severely disabled
pupils, but very difficult to meet the needs of those who are
physically intact and, apparently, within the normal intellectual
range. There are large numbers of pupils whose needs are not
being met; there are likely to be many more than a million pupils
with special needs according to the best available estimates:
"Given the wider concept of special education, some 20% of
children were likely to be in need of special educational provision
(rather than the 2% covered by the existing official definition of
special education)."[3]

This is the figure given in the Warnock Report and the one
accepted in the present book. It is highly probable that the
number of pupils is even higher, but a million is quite sufficient
for our initial consideration; these are pupils whose educational
needs are not being fully recognized, assessed or treated. Their
poor educational performance is strongly correlated with social
class, sex, ethnicity and region: working-class black boys from the
inner city areas are over-represented. By far the most significant
factor is the social class of the pupil and nothing much has
changed since the National Child Development Study presented
its findings so graphically in *11,000 Seven-year-olds*: "In children of
this age there is clear evidence that the lower the status of the
father's occupation, the poorer the reading achievement of the
children."[4]

Subsequent researches have shown that these class differences
had increased by the time the children were 11 years old. An
Inner London Educational Area (ILEA) survey[5] showed that at
age 10 there was a huge difference between the reading scores of
children from social class 1 ("professional") as compared with
those from social class V ("unskilled working class"): "Where
social disadvantage is high . . . the chances of success are in
general terms reduced, though even in the most disadvantaged
circumstances there are examples of success." Asking what else
might be done, the ILEA document responded: "Whilst our
education system remains unchanged, it is hard to see how a
major improvement in the achievement of children from working
class families could be brought about."

This analysis is supplemented by Monica Taylor's[6] review of research on the treatment of West Indian pupils: "... there is overwhelming consensus that research evidence shows a strong trend to under-achievement of pupils of West Indian origin on the main indicators of academic performance ... (they) are more likely to be found in the lower streams, much higher proportions in ESN (sic) schools and there appears to be evidence that they suffer stress in the school environment."

These are broad generalizations which will be related in this section to particular cases which illustrate the theme of the book. Although the generalizations are true within their own frame of reference, they are of little use to those who have to deal with the practical problems of "how to reach the hard to teach"; and there is a great danger that they will give rise to negative expectations in the minds of teachers and others who are professionally involved with young people. Much more interesting are the differences *within* the group and if we can put names to faces we shall be much less likely to create self-fulfilling prophecies. Within this group of pupils there is a considerable range of natural abilities, aptitudes and skills. They have been chosen as a cross-section of pupils who might be identified among the million manifesting special educational needs in our multicultural schools; they are certainly not a representative sample but their troubles make the point that educational needs are diverse and not to be easily resolved by slogans, or simple-minded "solutions". These pupils require understanding and patient, longterm help.

All the details in the following case studies are authentic, but names of persons and places have been fictionalized.

ANNE (15) was referred to the Child Guidance Service because of her difficult and aggressive behaviour in school. She had been suspended for short periods after displaying unacceptable behaviour such as throwing a stone at the physical education teacher. Her refusal to conform to the discipline of the school had been unaffected by all the usual methods: suspension, strapping, talking to. The headteacher thus felt that Anne was in need of some "cure" which was outside of the school's expertise and responsibility.

In small groups at the Child Guidance Service she talked easily but did seem to have a slight speech impediment, pronouncing, for example "fish" as "fizz". She said she was glad she had been expelled from school, because she hated it and the teachers there. She had been expelled because the teachers did not like her. She was, however, able to differentiate between them: one whom she hated particularly was a Mr K who had bad breath and breathed all over her when he was shouting at her. She said she had told him he had bad breath. She had thrown the stone at the physical education teacher because the teacher had called her "a little bitch" and had said that the school would be better off without her. In any case, she had only been trying to find a slide which had come out of her hair – she saw the slide and the stone, and picked up the stone and threw it, not *at* the teacher, but *near* the teacher: "anyway, she deserved it".

The teachers at school, when asked to give opinions, were almost unanimous in referring to her as a most disruptive girl "who displays an aggressive attitude when criticized and has a strange habit of smiling when being punished".

Anne's difficulties nearly all seemed to stem from her reactions to the authority structure of the school, as she had a close-knit, supportive home. Her learning difficulties were most apparent in reading. Her intelligence quotient as measured on the Weschler Intelligence Scale (W.I.S.C.) fell within the normal range, with her non-verbal quotient above her verbal quotient. She seemed to be a girl who wished to conform to the norms of her peer group and she had been placed in a class where there were many pupils who were resentful of authority; in many respects she was merely conforming to the sub-culture in which she was placed.

It proved possible to wean Anne from some of these behaviours and, through various forms of role play, to assist her to practise her responses to authority so that she was able to develop a more controlled and acceptable response in the real situation. After six weeks of "treatment" she was attending school full time, and although sometimes she looked pale and stressed, she persevered and did not become a school refuser.

PETER was one of twin boys. Measured against others in his year group, he was somewhat under-sized and under-weight, but of average height, with sandy coloured hair, blue eyes and freckles. His hair seemed to have been badly cut at home and he frequently needed a good wash. He always appeared unkempt and disheveled. His clothes were dirty and looked uncared for. Besides his twin brother, he had three older sisters, one younger sister and one younger brother. Peter freely volunteered the information that his parents had divorced two years ago: when drunk the father had beaten both mother and children. The father still saw the family occasionally. When Peter entered the school his reputation as a trouble maker had preceded him; the junior school headmaster, when commenting on his older sister, warned that "the worst one was still to come". On the whole, the junior school had labelled the family as a cause of trouble.

On the test given at entry to secondary school (Daniels and Diack *Reading Comprehension Test*) Peter revealed that he was effectively unable to read anything except the basic sight words such as "the, and, a". Further testing on a test provided by the National Foundation for Educational Research (*Non-verbal Reasoning Test DH*) showed that he had an intelligence quotient of 94, which placed him in the normal range and not as a candidate for a special school.

His behaviour was aggressive. He was always willing to finish off someone else's quarrel with a fight. He was openly defiant of authority and would shout across the classroom. Nevertheless, when Peter was closely observed during two thirty-minute science lessons he was helpful in giving out apparatus and appeared interested in the practical work on heating chemicals. He seemed quite absorbed in his work though he tended to be selfish with equipment and became the self-appointed leader of his group. Once his interest began to wane, he became playful; for example, he nipped a girl with tongs because she would not hand over a piece of apparatus. In a domestic science lesson, he was enthusiastic even though he lacked initiative, doubted his own ability and needed constant reassurance. He was always polite and concentrated on the task in hand such as rolling out the pastry. He remembered instructions from previous demonstration lessons which were pertinent to this particular lesson. He asked intelligent questions about necessary equipment and was not distracted.

Peter, it was concluded, was essentially a very unhappy boy. He was obviously motivated to learn when his interest was aroused and success was fairly painlessly achieved. However, he became bored easily and lost concentration when the tasks given him were beyond his current capabilities. There could be no doubt that he was most seriously handicapped by his low level of achievement in reading, which even after a period of intensive help, was still recorded at a reading age of 6 years 6 months. At least this did represent a fairly substantial gain when compared to his score on the original testing.

NARGIS BIBI, now aged 16, had come to England with her mother when she was 9 to join her father in a northern mill town. They lived in a house which he was buying on a mortgage and which they shared with another family, a cousin of Nargis's father. The family all spoke Punjabi and maintained regular contact with relatives in the Mirpur district in northern India, though Nargis had not returned to her homeland since her arrival in this country. In India, the family had lived in a small village, where Nargis's mother looked after the house and children. Like everyone in the village, they practised the Muslim religion; the women were very careful to place the *chaddar* over their heads when they left the house and only talked to people with whom they were acquainted. For a long time after they moved to England, Nargis's mother did not go out of the house at all.

Nargis quickly learned to read, write and speak English at a Language Centre. She did the shopping, made friends with English and Indian children, and was very happy. When she moved to the comprehensive school, she studied hard and was especially good at mathematics and science. It was expected that she would take 'O' and 'A' levels, and probably continue to study at a polytechnic or university. She was regarded as an ideal pupil, quick to learn, friendly, with a delightful personality that made her popular with almost everyone.

During her third year at the comprehensive school, a dramatic change occurred. Her attendance became irregular, she fell behind in her work and appeared to have lost interest. If questioned, she became withdrawn and refused to answer. She was referred to the Child Guidance Clinic, her father came to the school by request, but no explanation of her changed attitudes was elicited. The father seemed hostile and suspicious of the teachers, but was quite polite, and said very little.

Nargis made little further progress in school. She did not enter for any examinations and left as soon as she was legally entitled to do so. Shortly afterwards, it was learned that she had left home to avoid an arranged marriage. She was given a temporary home in a hostel for Asian girls and from there she asked to be allowed to return to school to take examinations. Her father was totally opposed to her continuing . . .

MICHAEL NEWBY[7] has published an account of his childhood learning difficulties.

My first realisation that I was having difficulty with work at school was when I found I could not understand my tables. I thereafter discovered, by sneaking glances at the written work of my fellows, that my writing was the worst in the class. In fact, it was almost wholly unreadable even by me, but up to then I had accepted my own work as the norm. I also found I was the only one in the class who did not know his ABC. I also muddled left and right.

There were some possible reasons for this condition, and he blamed particularly "troubles in the home". "I came to hate all adults, and school. I encouraged real illness where possible and invented illness whenever I could. I lied, cheated and withdrew from class work on every possible occasion. In class I refused to compete."

An undiagnosed visual defect further added to his learning difficulties. He became delinquent and destructive. His only outlets came through art. "The only praise I ever got was in art."

This state of affairs continued, worsening, until he was 15 and doing poorly in the 'C' stream. A friend began working for "promotion" to the next stream and "upset by the thought that I might lose him, because 'C' class boys rarely kept friends in other classes, I decided to go up with him." He suddenly began to concentrate on his work and excelled in the school examinations, to everyone's astonishment: "for once, I was the centre of attention". He went on, after a desperate struggle, to gain entry to the Slade School of Art and eventually entered the teaching profession.

ELDRIDGE was the youngest son of a Barbadian father and a Scots mother. He was born in the Gorbals district of Glasgow. His early childhood was decidedly unsettled, and he spent time alternately with his father in a city in north-west England and his mother in Glasgow, after the two had separated when he was 3 years of age. He was in care for a brief period when he was 5 after his mother had left him and his younger brother in a telephone box (following a serious disagreement between the parents). The two boys returned to Glasgow and remained there until Eldridge was seven, when his mother was murdered in his presence. The boys were taken into care for a few months until the father brought them to the north-west. Here he was co-habiting with a woman whom he married shortly after the children joined them; but the relationship deteriorated after a year or so, and Eldridge's father left to live with a nurse, a relationship which lasted for four years. She appeared to make every effort to stabilize the home situation, and there was an improvement in the boys' social behaviour and reaction to learning situations.

Eventually, the father left the nurse taking Eldridge and his elder brother with him, leaving her with a younger half brother – "a product of the co-habitation", as the case notes succinctly express it. Eldridge and his brother were now taken into the care of the social services and Eldridge was placed in a family group home, attending secondary school as a day pupil. They were removed into care at the request of the father and his most recent co-habitee, because of an inability on their part to control the behaviour of the two boys.

In school, Eldridge was referred by an English teacher for remedial treatment in spelling and written English. Not surprisingly, in view of his personal history, he revealed on the *Bristol Social Adjustment Guide* an extremely high score on the "inconsequence" scale (a measure of self-prediction and control of behaviour). A high score indicates "a failure to inhibit the first impulses for long enough for their consequences to be foreseen". He was, however, a competent reader, and one can only marvel at the resilience of the human capacity for learning. He had a ready comprehension of what he read and his difficulties appeared to be confined to spelling and handwriting. A remarkable finding was that he did *not* appear to have a poor self-image; what he did feel was that he was being singled out for criticism, and this particular belief arose from his having been withdrawn from the normal classroom into remedial groups. His written work showed imagination but he obviously found the physical effort of putting pen to paper very exacting, and it was decided to concentrate efforts to help him in these areas.

ALLAN came to the notice of his tutor in an upper school in a social priority area because he showed little sign of improvement, although he was receiving help on a withdrawal basis. When first admitted to the school he had had a reading age of 7 years 5 months (Daniels and Diack *Reading Comprehension Test*) while his chronological age was 13 years 3 months, one of the youngest in his year group. He was also physically smaller than most pupils and rather clumsy in his movements. He had a slight speech defect and a tendency to slur, and his diction was neither very clear nor well organized. His behaviour, compared with the rest of his class, appeared immature; he was innocent and unaware, and in the normal classroom seemed rather withdrawn and unresponsive, contributing very little to the lesson, and seemingly "switched off" or in a day-dream. In a small room, in a group of six, his behaviour changed quite drastically, and he played boyish pranks such as hiding under the table, making childish noises or joining in an argument.

His family background was anything but conducive to learning to read. His mother was Czechoslovakian and had come to Britain as a refugee at the end of the Second World War. She could not read or write English, although she understood and spoke the language fluently, with very little trace of an accent. Allan's father was British and literate, but worked on a night shift (semi-skilled) six nights a week. At weekends, he went shooting with his friends from work, or to the pub; both parents worked and Allan saw his father only for a short period in the evening before he left for work. Although the mother was at home every evening, she felt she could do nothing to help him with his reading. Allan's only sibling was a sister one year older, and in the fourth year of the same school. She was in a "A" band and appeared to be the pride and joy of the family, but this admiration had the effect of depressing Allan's self-image. She occasionally helped Allan with his reading but both quickly tired and became intolerant and short-tempered; he felt his sister talked down to him and lacked patience.

Allan talked readily about his learning difficulties. At his last school, he complained, his teachers took little interest in helping him with his reading and he frequently got lost or left behind, so that his concentration would wander, bringing him into further conflict with the teacher. Remedial sessions, which took place while the other pupils were having English lessons, consisted primarily of non-reading activities such as watching TV, drawing or playing games. He mentioned that he was frequently tired during the day and found it difficult to keep his attention on the task in hand; that he had headaches, particularly in a hot or stuffy room or in strong sunlight; and that he had difficulty in sleeping at night. He did not appear to have many interests and spent most evenings watching TV. He did keep a ferret and displayed a keen interest in ferreting. He was motivated to read and beginning to relate quite well to his remedial teacher. He appeared to be below average intelligence on non-verbal tests (such as Raven's *Matrices*). He revealed a possible hearing problem and when this was investigated, there did appear to be a defect. Words which to Allan sounded the same were: "can-cab"; "thief-sheaf"; "sake-shake"; "bead-deed"; "love-lath"; "last-laugh"; "gold-goad"; "thumb-done", "cuff-cuss", and so on.

Although LINCOLN AND ROGER were both second generation blacks of Caribbean culture, they had sharply different perceptions of their secondary schools, and after only five months were already well set on alternative careers.

These two boys were among a group I came to know when I studied a "successful", multicultural primary school (ages 5–11), and whom I subsequently followed when they transferred to secondary education at the age of about 11 years. I talked to them about their new school and how they felt about the learning situations with which they were now presented. About the only common element in their observations was that neither so much as mentioned the school buildings or facilities, which were solid, light, airy, in an excellent state of repair, and formed the main topic of conversation when I talked to the headteacher.

Roger had no difficulty in settling in to Bishdon High School because his brother had already been there and he knew quite a few pupils before he arrived. He had adapted completely to life at Bishdon. He was wearing a merit badge; he was immaculately turned out in full uniform; he spoke fluently, was friendly and relaxed and appeared happy, and was obviously progressing well within the framework provided by the school. He spoke about some subjects specifically, mentioning French, Science and English. He was taking part in the activities of the school brass band, and his trumpet-playing figured prominently in the school brochure. He talked at some length about the MACOS pro-gramme, which he found "a bit like science". (*MAN – a course of study* is a humanities course originally developed under the direction of Professor Jerome Bruner.) It was obvious from our conversation that this was a boy who was an enthusiastic partici-pant in the school programme as he found it. He seemed committed to academic goals and was making progress in a conventional sense.

Lincoln also mentioned MACOS, French and Science. To him, MACOS was "like History and Geography put together". He commented that discipline in the MACOS classes was good, but generally the class was rather noisy and difficult to control. We talked specially about these difficulties because Lincoln was in trouble at the time due to a row he had had with a teacher the day before. He had had the strap six times since arriving at the school (about five months before the interview); he admitted that he had been in some trouble at his primary school, but this seemed to have escalated sharply since he arrived at Bishdon. One way in which the trouble seemed to grow was through the establishment of a class norm for poor work, so that "if you worked, the others called you a creep". Lincoln claimed to have an interest in a number of school subjects, and to like games, but not to be able to apply himself to academic work because this would have put him outside acceptable class norms. He did not think that pupils from his primary school played any greater or lesser part than anyone else in establishing these norms. He was not a member of any gang led by the chief troublemaker, Freddy Mahon. He described his antipathy to authority in terms of: "If a teacher shouts at you, I shout back". The previous day's episode had involved his being hauled out and put against the wall, objecting to the teacher placing his hands on him (Lincoln) and knocking these away. Lincoln was obviously at odds with authority.

He explained that the games he liked to play with his friends in the playground were "tiggy" and football. Of these friends, he met only one out of school. He was slightly above average height for his age, and gave the impression of being strong and about to grow into a large person. He played in school cricket and football teams and in conversation with me he was friendly, speaking coherently, though quietly. When he talked about his troubles with teachers, he was in no sense repentant. He talked in a matter-of-fact voice as if to be in trouble were an inevitable part of school experience, and not as if he felt that he was particularly singled out as a trouble maker, even though he was one of those punished most frequently. He too was wearing a merit badge, representing twenty-five credits on various subjects. He seemed to think it fairly easy to earn a merit badge, but quite clearly indicated through this and through his membership of school footbal and cricket teams that his desire to co-operate was by no means negligible. In his version of events, others paved the way, and the general indiscipline of the classes produced a situation in which he, as one reluctant to accept adult authority, tended to drift into difficulties. As soon as he was confronted by a teacher he would offer a resistance, which threatened the school ethos.

When the first year master returned to the room and joined in the conversation it became apparent that he was not aware that Lincoln played in school teams. I mentioned that the boy played a guitar and that to encourage him to contribute to school music-making might be a way of achieving a positive approach to his behaviour problems. This was not taken up. Lincoln was clearly known as a trouble maker and the beginnings of a spiral of antisocial behaviour, leading to a falling-off in attainment, could be easily discerned. The first year master mentioned Lincoln's older brother in the third year, commenting that he too, had never settled, "though your mother does her best for you, doesn't she?"

It is clear that Lincoln already had a reputation through his brother before he ever entered the school, and rapidly gave evidence that it was justified. Even the headteacher had heard of Lincoln, commenting that he and Roger were the two she had first been told about, and for opposite reasons. Lincoln, on this evidence, was already one of the 20 per cent of pupils in British State schools manifesting special educational needs. Very fre-quently, their difficulties will be compounded by behaviour like that of Lincoln's; but in his case, the behaviour seemed to be the core.

A study by Paul Willis[8] also identified two main groups of boys in schools, conformist and non-conformist. The latter group contained mainly boys of average to low ability (in terms of achievement) who were not going to get paper qualifications on leaving school, and who were destined for basic unskilled or semi-skilled jobs. In their own terminology the groups were the "lads" and the "ear 'oles". The "lads" largely either rejected the overt aims of schooling and legitimacy of teachers to guide them or were deeply ambiguous about what they thought the school was trying to do – mainly it boiled down to "pushing us around".

The "ear 'oles" largely took the school on its own terms and accepted the legitimacy of the teachers. The "lads" regarded them as "creeps", "arse creepers", "teachers' pets" and despised them for their conformity to school norms, for their lack of assertiveness, for their inability to show any autonomy, and most of all for their inability to create "fun" for themselves, to "have a laff".

The "lads'" opposition to the school and its agents, and their scornful rejection of the "ear 'oles" – not least because of their acceptance of the legitimacy of the school – were very powerful determinants of what amounted to an anti-school, alternative, or counter-culture within the school. Membership of this culture, or their relationship to it, was very much more important to the non-academic working-class lads than was the achievement of any formal aims of education, or the satisfaction of any other independent or "free" form of social education. It was the "spine" around which their day and thoughts were organized: the dichotomy "lads"/"ear 'oles" was the most basic organizing structure of school life.

Roger was already an "ear 'ole", Lincoln a "lad", though they had barely settled in to their new secondary school. It was quite obvious to an experienced observer that the school's response to Lincoln's behaviour was not producing or likely to produce its intended result. Lincoln would not become more conformist but, instead, would increasingly contract out of a system which to him seemed remote and alien. Such pupils observe the education scene in something like the same spirit as football pool punters during the summer months when Australian teams are used as a substitute for the English league; the game is familiar and they know the rules; they want to win but have no chance of acquiring the inside knowledge necessary to ensure a reasonable hope of success; the result matters enormously but it is all slightly unreal, impersonal – antipodean. The poor quality of the relationship which these pupils have with educational institutions is a very potent source of low attainment.

The authoritarian stance adopted by such schools towards the community as well as their pupils is, to put it bluntly, totally inappropriate to the changed and changing educational circumstances outlined in Chapter 2.

References

1. *Schools Council News*, Spring 1981, Holt Park Middle School.
2. HEGARTY S. and POCKLINGTON K. (1982) *Integration in Action: Case Studies in the Integration of Pupils with Special Educational Needs*, NFER/Nelson.
3. *Special Educational Needs (The Warnock Report)* (1978) HMSO.
4. PRINGLE, M.L.Kellmer, BUTLER, N.R. and DAVIE, R. (1966) *11,000 Seven-Year-Olds*, Longmans.
5. Inner London Education Authority (1981) *Achievement in Schools 1: Social Class* Research and Statistics Report 805/81.
6. TAYLOR, M. (1981) *Caught Between*, NFER/Nelson.
7. NEWBY, M. (1977) "Case History of a backward child" in WIDLAKE, P. (ed) (1977) *Remedial Education: Programmes and Progress*, Longman/NARE.
8. WILLIS, P. (1977) *Learning to Labour: How Working Class Kids Get Working Class Jobs*, Saxon House, Farnborough.

CHAPTER 2

Changing Schools to Reach the Hard to Teach

The case for change

It will have hurt many teachers that John Holt,[1] whose earlier books on why children fail in schools were much admired, has now come to feel that satisfactory conditions for learning can rarely be achieved within a public service and has begun urging parents to keep their children away altogether and to educate them at home. It is easy to understand this position, but the case studies already quoted have shown that many pupils *do* receive sympathetic support – though too often the reasons why they require it have been generated by the schools themselves. The point is, surely, that whatever the difficulties, schools must be made better places in which to learn. Ninety-six per cent of the population attend state schools and for them there is no effective alternative. Instead of romanticizing about de-schooling, it is important to answer the straightforward questions: what can be done to ensure that the excellence to be found in a large number of British schools can be replicated everywhere and that the performance of the best teachers can become more nearly the norm for the profession as a whole? For despite everything that has been said against it, the system functions reasonably well; valuable empirical evidence of the effectiveness of secondary schools has been provided by Rutter and his colleagues.[2] But the truth is that schools in some parts of the system are held together by a relatively small group of well-above-average professionals. This works well enough until social and political events combine to worsen conditions, and then it is but a small step to disaster. After all, we *have* experienced riots – primary school pupils running amok and setting fire to their classrooms.

14

It is therefore apparent that schools cannot continue to function as if they were insulated from society. Every event in a pupil's life may have some bearing on his or her capacity to learn. When "normal" individuals show an inability to learn in school, yet are perfectly capable of learning in other situations, one should be driven to consider what aspects of society are creating negative attitudes to school and whether changes are necessary in the schools themselves. It is obvious that attempts to treat learning difficulties cannot be confined to more and more intensive work with individuals, however desirable it is to increase our understanding of, and empathy with, particular pupils. Yet this seems to be the direction of many special education programmes in ordinary schools which offer, for example, intensive language "development" based on a teacher-provided, American originated programme such as DISTAR, instead of encouraging the use of language appropriate to school learning and personal growth. I want to argue in favour of these pupils being given access to as much of the content of a "normal" curriculum as is compatible with their skills and abilities and, where there seems any doubt, to err on the side of expecting too much rather than too little.

Teachers who have specialized in treating learning difficulties sometimes appear to be fearful that their own skills will become redundant if such integration is practised. A dynamic example to the contrary is the UNESCO World Literacy Project[3] which started from the writings of Paulo Freire,[4] the Brazilian educator who has developed a method that "helps illiterates to awake from their lethargy and to participate, as subjects, in the development of their countries". Methods which recognize the social context of learning actually extend the scope of specialist teachers and ultimately raise their status, even though at first they may seem to pose a threat. Schools must change, then, if they are to meet special educational needs in the last two decades of the twentieth century. There is an inner dynamic, as has been shown, deriving from the urgent, unmet needs of individual pupils. But there are other fundamental changes in the structure of society which affect everyone and cannot be ignored by teachers if they are to have any credibility with their pupils.

The two changes which most obviously impinge on schools are the rapid increase in unemployment, especially among school leavers; and the technology and communications revolution. The former has "backlash" effects upon the curriculum and the kind of preparation for life which the school aims to provide; the latter already has an influence on the methods adopted by teachers,

Figure 2.1   Some change agents in contemporary multicultural British society

Family Structure	"Nuclear" family (F+M+2C) no longer the only model; divorce rate increased nearly 400 per cent since 1971; many child-rearing situations – single parent; dual rather than single worker families; re-constituted families (involving step-brothers and sisters, step-parents/ families with adopted or fostered parents); extended families.
Employment	Changes in job content and locations; slower entry; earlier retirement; fewer hours; more training; structural unemployment affecting especially school leavers.
Increased Tension	Experience of breakdowns in law and order; increased crime rate; disaffection of minority groups.
Leisure	More disposable time available even for employed people; enforced "leisure" for unemployed.
Technology and Communications	Television and videotape machines; computers provide alternative learning systems to schools; the "new knowledge" explosion.

and this increases by the week. Schools are no longer the only source of learning; videorecorders and personal computers (and the learning possibilities they provide) are as commonly found in the home as in the classroom.

In the home many children are being reared under conditions other than the nuclear unit of father, mother and one or two children. The fact that they do not conform to some idealized pattern does not mean that they are necessarily "problem" families but clearly an understanding of the new conditions is an essential prerequisite for any teacher who hopes to help pupils with special needs.

Any one of the changes listed in Fig 2.1, occurring at the pace characteristic of the late twentieth century, would be difficult to accommodate; taken together, they tend to induce "future shock" among the teachers who bear the brunt of trying to adapt schools to the constantly expanding body of knowledge and to diverse and sometimes contradictory demands from parents, employers and politicians.

The challenges from within and without are such that no school can continue to teach its present curriculum in an unchanged form. There seems little evidence that this message is being received with regard to pupils with special needs. Dead, dry-as-dust, irrelevant material continues to be taught by boring and incompetent methods (this has been shown by Brennan, quoted in Chapter 4). Didactic methods which induce passivity on the learner's part, and which refer to other pupils' norms rather than to personal criteria, are unlikely to produce students with the necessary qualities for survival in the eighties and nineties. Everyone *says* this, but examples of methodologies which really get to grips with not-very-cooperative young people are quite rare. This is the theme of the present book. How to reach Eldridge and Anne and Allan and the rest; how to provide them with the educational regime which will enable them to grow up into flexible and adaptable citizens, able and willing to continue learning, able to work alone but also in teams, able to make constructive use of substantial periods of leisure and to cope with the prospect of being unemployed.

To move towards such provision, the curriculum should be dominated by four principles:

1. Education is a process which continues throughout life.
2. There should be open access to a wide range of educational choices and opportunities.
3. There should be provision for building individual competence and skills.
4. The educational process should promote self-confidence and self-awareness.

To these ends the curriculum for pupils with special needs should be transformed. To stand a realistic chance of success, attempts toward change must recognize:

(a) It is necessary and desirable to obtain relevant, usable information about the learning difficulties of all pupils with special educational needs, and to arrange for individualized learning programmes for those pupils.
(b) It is not, however, sufficient to treat the pupil on an individual basis. Pupils are members of a multicultural society and subject to the same opportunities and stresses as everyone else.

This has clear implications for the selection of curriculum content and for methods.

(c) The pupil has to learn within the organization of the school, with all the values of its hidden curriculum. These are sometimes more important in determining whether learning occurs than the overt arrangements and must, therefore, also be considered.

Making the change

Schools which act as if their walls were as thick as those of a medieval castle will find that their pupils come to consider them as being just about as relevant to their preparation for life in multicultural, twentieth century Britain. The position adopted by schools which try to exist in isolation from the community they serve is no longer tenable and is, in fact, rarely defended; but lip-service is not enough – there has to be some real exchange, some direct involvement by parents, some bargaining about the limits of professional responsibility, some mutual give and take. None of this is easy to achieve, but many schools have been remarkably successful in removing their physical or mental barriers against the community without loss of confidence in the school's academic standard. This is a very hard task indeed, one that requires the highest level of personal and managerial skills. Nevertheless, schools which are mainly preoccupied with matters of discipline, which are inward-looking and institution-oriented, cannot consider solutions which demand trust, openness to new ideas, inputs from other professions. The level of debate is still comparatively basic. For example, there are hard-liners who maintain that corporal punishment is a necessary deterrent in schools. I have heard the argument along the following lines:

> You have to care enough to suppress your own distaste, to say that it may not be likeable but it is necessary, and that is what most parents have to face up to. Heads too frequently wish to espouse liberal philosophies, possibly to please the pink-spectacled people on the Education Committee, with total disregard for the practicalities of the school.

Where are these heads, one wonders, and who appoints them? Certainly Geoff Lawes, a comprehensive school headmaster, rejected corporal punishment on the grounds that it is unethical, unprofessional and useless:

> I am against caning because I believe in discipline. My job is to shape gentle, self-disciplined people. But I cannot gain worthy ends by unworthy means – I have to convince children to behave well, not intimidate them through fear. In the hidden curriculum

of the caning school is the message that authority depends upon the power to inflict pain . . . schools should present a model of the best practices of society and not rely on an anachronistic code like that of Nelson's navy . . .[5]

Nevertheless, corporal punishment is still widespread in British schools, contrary to popular belief. In his autobiography Trevor Brooking, the international footballer, expressed the view that "the cane will have to be used again in schools" if football hooliganism is to be cured. In a subsequent letter (*The Guardian*, 10 December 1982) Paul Temperton pointed out:

There are two weaknesses in this statement. Firstly, the implied premise that caning has already been banished from schools is wildly incorrect, and secondly, the notion that corporal punishment improves behaviour is contradicted by a wealth of education research and practical experience. Eighty per cent of British schools retain corporal punishment. Only six local authorities have so far banned it. We estimate on the basis of official LEA statistics, that in England alone, there are about a quarter of a million recorded beatings every year; and from what records are available it is clear that quite a few schools use the cane lavishly. Thus, the great majority of football hooligans must come from caning schools.

Many schools still seem to regard the process of abolishing corporal punishment as a major event and as late as 1981, the Scottish Council for Research in Education (SCRE) published a booklet *Making the change*[6] which offered the reassurance that in schools which had given up corporal punishment wholly or substantially teaching and learning went on as elsewhere. This indicates the degree of apprehension felt by many teachers at the loss of their main sanction but unless a school can pass beyond this primitive stage, there is really no possibility of an adequate response to special educational needs. The absurdity of schoolmasters (and mistresses?) attempting to use corporal punishment on an age group stretching from 11 to 18 years hardly requires stating and this applies not only to the cane but to many other of the twenty sanctions listed by the SCRE report. (Figure 2.2)

Such "sanctions", boldly expressed in this manner, seem more likely to produce confrontation than co-operation from the students and ultimately some form of agreement has to be negotiated with the vast majority; no matter what measures are taken against those who will not – or cannot – conform to school protocol, these should not be allowed to become the norms for the school as a whole. A civilized atmosphere has to be created. Parents should be involved *before* a crisis arises. Teachers should cultivate "enabling skills". (Figure 2.3)

---

*Figure 2.2   Sanctions employed: A composite list indicating a
trend in seriousness*

1. Non-verbal cues, silences, disapproving gestures.
2. Rebukes, tellings off, to individual, group, class.
3. Lines, extra homework, punishment exercises, unproductive writing.
4. Threat of movement to other seat in class.
5. Movement of seat.
6. Threat of isolation in another class.
7. Time-out, "on-assignment", isolation.
8. Detention, unofficial, in class teacher's room.
9. Corporal punishment.
10. Threat of report, oral or in writing, to guidance or Year Head or "Office".
11. Report and possible intervention by Year Head and guidance.
12. Withdrawal of privilege.
13. Official detention, school-organized.
14. Threat of parental involvement.
15. On report: behaviour timetables with or without parental knowledge.
16. Letter or telephone call to parents informing of problem.
17. Pupil sent home for clarification (a pre-suspension warning).
18. Parental involvement through visit to school.
19. Withdrawal to Special Unit.
20. Tactical or unofficial suspension.
21. Suspension, exclusion – official.

Source: *Making the change*. Scottish Council for Research in Education.

What makes a good school

Rutter (1980)[8] and his colleagues have conducted a study which
conforms to many teachers' definition of the purpose of educational research: it provides firm, empirical evidence for what
everyone knew all along! They have proved that schools which
function efficiently, which care about their students and provide
proper conditions for learning, get better examination results and
have better-behaved students than those where the staff have less
grip and care less. It is not all that much of a surprise that Rutter
and his colleagues have found "large and important differences
between secondary schools in each measure of pupil success or
outcome, even after all possible due allowance had been made for
variations between the schools in the proportions of behaviour-

---

Figure 2.3   Enabling skills

Secondary schools can achieve little if an "us or them" situation is created between pupils and teachers. A diagnosis of difficulties and a prescriptive programme are of little value unless there is a "contract" between child, parent and teacher that ensures the willingness of all parties to work together. Too many diagnoses and prescriptions remain like descriptive labels on a collection of shelved bottles.

Maslow (1970)[7] has described a sound relationship as one in which the people do not have to defend themselves. Within the relationship between the teacher and the disturbed child this means that the teacher is not continually being affronted by maladaptive behaviour nor forcing confrontations; rather he/she seeks to avoid such make or break situations, by becoming aware of the behaviour patterns of the pupils. A quarrel begun in the playground and carried simmering into the classroom may be defused in many ways. Teachers might begin the classwork from the chair next to the most disturbed party to the quarrel, using as an introduction a class joke against themselves – knowing that in this situation laughter will reduce the tension.

Mental preparation, observing behaviour patterns, understanding the language appropriate to each child: these are necessary skills for teachers of disturbed children. They are enabling skills. Through their use the teacher is able to create an interrelationship with the children in the classroom and ensure that together they form a unified team. Ideas on acceptable classroom behaviour are "contracted" between teacher and class. Cooling-off areas, quiet areas, work areas: such arrangements can only be established and underwritten by the teacher's enabling skills.

The process of establishing a caring relationship can be summarized as follows:

Define what is wanted in terms of class behaviour.

Listen, observe, use the appropriate language or dialect of the child.

Prepare responses in advance. Defuse whenever possible.

Avoid confrontations, for nobody wins such battles, least of all the teacher.

Create a team where neither the teacher nor the pupils feel a need to defend themselves.

---

ally difficult, socially disadvantaged or low attaining pupils on roll. The differences between schools also could not be accounted for in terms of the variations in the schools' catchment areas." Of course, such analyses beg many questions, and are severely criticized as "functionalist" by more radical sociologists. They accept the school system much as it is and ignore the policy decisions which have delivered particular populations to particular schools. Even so, this research has pushed back the frontier of pessimism by some distance, and it goes on to identify features of schools which promote this kind of success. Even the most radical critic might agree that schools, since they do exist (and at great public expense) might as well be as good as possible. They will not achieve this, according to Rutter's analysis, by concentrating on matters pertaining to resources, organizational structure and punishment – all very much to the forefront when school failure is being discussed. Certain features fostering pupil success were singled out. (Figure 2.4)

To these features may be added many others, and there are some value judgements which certainly do require further discussion (such as "academic emphasis") in the light of the very different circumstances obtaining in the eighties. An "ethnographic" study of a school conducted by Madeleine Piper and myself[9] indicated some similar features to those of Rutter: consistency in transmission of values, high expectations, continuity between teachers over curriculum, but threw the emphasis on other aspects:

– a humourous and caring atmosphere
  (Humour seems too often to be left out of these discussions)
– openness – frankness in discussing errors and difficulties.

Everyone, teachers and pupils, ought to be able to discuss difficulties without feeling that the admission will be damaging, or will be seized upon and used as a weapon to gain an advantage. Some specialist schools, like the Royal Ballet School, create a spirit of ruthless self-criticism which is accepted by everyone and is highly productive, rather than pathological as can happen when the criticism is in one direction only.

Such schools also exist, though not in very large numbers, in the state system. They manage to establish a milieu within which it is natural that decision-making involves all the staff, so that teachers feel that their views are represented and seriously considered. This was one of the factors in organizational style which Rutter found to be associated with pupil success.

Recently, I took part in a one-day conference with the whole

Figure 2.4   Features promoting success in schools

Rewards and Praise
Frequent public praise, and commendation of individual pupils is associated with good behaviour.

Pupil Conditions
A pleasant and comfortable environment is associated with better pupil outcomes – *not* school buildings or small classes but:
– good decorations and care of buildings
– freedom to use them during breaks
– availability of hot drinks
– outings
– availability of teachers.

Responsibilities and Participation
Giving pupils opportunities to take responsibilities and to participate in running the school is conducive to good attainments, attendance and behaviour.

Academic Emphasis
Pupils make better progress when clear goals are set and where there is an atmosphere of confidence that they can and will succeed in the tasks set.

Models Provided by Teachers
Pupils copy teacher behaviour:
– punctuality
– negative reactions to provocation.

Group Management in the Classroom
Pupil behaviour is better when:
– lessons are prepared in advance
– pupils are kept actively engaged in productive activities
– there is unobtrusive discipline: not shouting but swift action to deal with disruption when necessary.

Staff Organization
Pupil outcomes are better when both curriculum and approaches to discipline are agreed and supported by staff acting together.

---

staff of a community school in the East Midlands. I was impressed by their professionalism, self-criticial but constructive attitudes and the caring qualities they displayed towards their pupils. The conference was called to review their policies towards language work – in areas of the curriculum other than English – and towards involving parents. It was an encouraging day because the staff were not defensive; they defined their continuing difficulties and were looking, collectively, at existing practices with the intention of modifying them if necessary. It seemed a far cry from the anxiety-ridden traumas of those schools where they are still fixated on punishment and suppression; it is not really feasible to think along those latter lines in a community school.

Community schools

What is most heartening about schools which have adopted a community approach, is their enthusiasm, willingness to experiment, to weld new ideas on to older structures and to offer educational opportunities to the widest possible audience, including adults. Teachers in these schools do not spend much time lamenting the poor quality of the intake or the lack of motivation of their pupils; their energies are directed towards creating a suitable learning environment and ensuring its continuity. It does not follow that a community school is the only form of schooling that can achieve this, but it is very difficult to envisage any educational establishment surviving over the next two decades which does not adopt a positive attitude to the notion of life-long learning and to a genuine involvement with the community it serves.

Henry Morris[10] first conceived the idea of "village colleges" in Cambridgeshire in the 1920s. A network of community colleges has been established throughout that county, Sawston (the first), Sawtry, Impington, Bottisham, Witchford, Ely, Bushfield. . . . The list is long and indicates the continuing commitment on the part of that Local Education Authority to the Community College ideal.

The Cambridgeshire village colleges set out to ensure the full use of their premises by community groups and adults learning in various formal and informal ways. But some have gone much further. Bushfield Community Campus, for example, is an amalgam of an 11 to 16 community school, a district library and a district sports centre, situated in the middle of the shopping and administrative Orton centre, a new township of Peterborough. The campus buildings existed before the community. In the early stages the immediate environment consisted of empty houses and untenanted factory units, while the nearest settled housing was two and a half miles away, and only two years old, inhabited by people coming from all points of the compass, preoccupied with the basic business of coping with their new homes, laying out gardens and foraging for shops.

> We had to plan something for them. In retrospect, however, we have done those things best which were based on an instinctive, and I trust, sensitive, response to expressed needs of the people we have got to know as friends, sometimes as enemies.[11]

A host of Bushfield clubs were set up by enthusiasts for their own benefit, but they soon open-heartedly welcomed all. A thriving Friends of Bushfield Association has launched out into an Orton Youth Action Project to build a Youth Centre, organize an annual Festival of the Arts and act as a ginger group to provide such diverse amenities as bus stops for the elderly, toilets for the disabled and to criticize the patronage of *nouveau art* sculpture in the square!

The community schools which have attracted the most attention have tended to be those which were purpose built, which began with a coherent educational philosophy and which had supportive local authorities helping prepare the local community for this style of secondary education. However, even with local authority support, Countesthorpe in Leicestershire and Sutton Centre in Nottinghamshire (two community schools which have existed in a blaze of publicity from the beginning) have both experienced traumatic periods in their development and aroused considerable opposition from local minority groups of parents. There is an inherent source of controversy in community schools in that the very opening up and extension of educational opportunities seems to some parents to threaten the reduction of opportunities for the most able – they fear that academic standards will be lost in all the "frills". Less seems to be heard from the parents of pupils with other educational needs, but these schools certainly make a determined effort to provide appropriate educational programmes for pupils of all abilities.

There are now many good examples of urban community schools. For instance, Blakelaw was a split-site comprehensive school which drew its pupils mainly from three Newcastle suburbs: Fenham, Blakelaw and Carrol Gate. The areas were very different. The first contained some of the poorest housing estates in the city, to which, inevitably, many problem families migrated. The second contained a mixture of private housing and pleasant, "older council houses". The third contained attractive new council houses and high rise flats in a pleasantly landscaped area. The community was a geographical area only. Houses and families

were linked only by roads and roundabouts. People worked in
the city rather than in the suburbs although it was an area of high
unemployment, with a high incidence of one-parent families and
much overt and hidden poverty:

> But within its estates and streets and houses, live people with
> common aims for themselves and their children and grand-
> children, common hopes for the future and common difficulties,
> problems and needs. When we talk about our "community" in
> inverted commas we're not just thinking of a generation which is
> currently in the school's classrooms but of all the people in our
> catchment area.

Blakelaw had not at the time of this description been designated as a community school, and so there was no money directly
available for a development programme; nevertheless, staff felt
that this particular school, in this particular area, should "open its
doors" to the community and they developed what they called an
"Outreach Programme." This in essence was an attempt to
produce the maximum interaction possible between school and
community with the minimum of expenditure – only about £3,000
in grants was available:

> The school has always placed a high priority on pastoral care,
> home liaison, parent/teacher relationships, social education and
> community service. We have always been in one sense a neigh-
> bourhood or community school, but our energies were directed
> mainly towards the children currently in school and their fami-
> lies.[12]

The programme has incorporated a community newspaper, a
summer festival, curriculum work involving community resources, and specifically, the establishment of a community wing
containing three large rooms, links area and toilets, which was
staffed by three workers from the Community Enterprise Project,
assisted by one parent who is unemployed. There was at the time
of writing no full-time trained community worker but five members of school staff were directly involved in supervising and
manning individual activities, which included a playgroup, a
mother and toddler group, badminton, craft sessions, whist,
bingo, junior club, listening post (counselling service), sessions
with the young unemployed, a visiting service for housebound
old people and a Monday Club (parents' social and educational
meeting).

There is a welter of experimental programmes and particular
initiatives being developed all over the country so there are

models for schools which wish to take this path. Yet the community school movement has not grown rapidly. For the most part, schools follow their traditional pattern with the curriculum having little relationship to the ideal of education continuing beyond school; adult, youth, and school management are separated at the level of the local authority and even within the community/school centre. How then, does a school go about changing its character?

Changing a school's character

Quintin Kynaston[13] is a mixed comprehensive school in North London drawing pupils from St John's Wood, Paddington, Queen's Park and Camden Town. The school became a comprehensive boys' school in 1969 and a mixed school in 1976. Over four years it has been organizing the curriculum so that courses emphasize the learning process. This is partly to support mixed ability grouping, which is used in all courses for the first three years, and partly to prepare people for continuing with their studies beyond school. Describing the process, the Headteacher recounts how the first paper describing the community education centre called for facilities which were far too radical to be taken seriously as a proposal; but it did open a debate among staff, parents and governors on the possibilities of community education expanding the educational opportunities on the Quintin Kynaston site and within the community. The staff and a group of parent governors set up a joint working party, to prepare a paper to the ILEA. This focused on the integration of compulsory school and voluntary youth activities which are usually managed separately. It was argued that bringing these together would enable pupils to volunteer for activities which would complement, extend and contrast with their work in school which they inevitably saw as compulsory and unavoidable. Voluntary educational activities would cater for the 11–21 age group. They would run from the end of school until 10 at night and be open to pupils from other schools. Local community groups would be involved in setting up and managing these voluntary activities. The whole process took three years which was: *"A marvellous opportunity to think through a consistent educational philosophy for 11–21 year olds"*.

A school which has taken the process some stages further is Craigroyston in Edinburgh. This is of particular interest because the processes by which the school has been developing itself into a community school have been closely monitored with the aid of a grant from the Van Leer Foundation. Documents are available which demonstrate how a school staff can engage in this difficult transition. In setting the scene for the transition, the school identified the main problems as follows:

> Within the community, school was viewed as an alien institution – not least by parents who transmitted this attitude to their children – and there was no tradition of voluntary education beyond the legal school-leaving age; most students were lacking in self-esteem and regarded themselves as outside the academic category for whom they believed schools catered; the lack of access to cultural and recreational activities meant that students were isolated within the narrow limits of their impoverished community; the absence of good adult models for many students resulted in immature and socially unacceptable behaviour; the socially vicious circle in which the students lived meant limited choices for them in regard to their future life-styles.[14]

The Craigroyston curriculum aimed to enable every student to develop capability, confidence, co-operativeness and caring attitudes and attempted to do this by adding a number of elements to normal Scottish education. The chosen method by which the school has set about implementing this expansion of its interests was through a series of eleven working parties, each of which was given responsibility for a different part of the evolving community–school relationship. One working party looked after *Commune*, a monthly community newspaper produced and delivered to 10,000 households; another was concerned with the learning centre, which provided hardware and software to meet the educational needs of the more able student, and students (later "people") with learning difficulties; others dealt with out-of-door activities, lifelong learning, the under-fives and so on.

A very thorough work-plan was prepared and each working party kept full Minutes of its meetings. They placed particular emphasis on aims and objectives and noted any re-statements of objectives giving reasons for the change and details of the way in which it was effected. The Minutes are refreshingly frank and record failures as well as successes. It proved more difficult than was expected to involve adults from the community in "outdoor/residential education" and "design for living"; but the lifelong education programme was extremely successful in recruiting adult students to day school classes. The Second Year Work-Plan built on the successes and attempted to remedy the failures. The project is being evaluated by the Scottish Council for Research in Education. Another document which will be essential reading for anyone involved in planning a transition towards a community school has been produced by the Community Education Development Centre.[11]

It is, of course, possible to move toward community schooling without undertaking such massive changes. For instance, North Westminster Community School, which serves the families and communities in a large part of Marylebone and Paddington and beyond, seems to be striking an effective middle course. An eloquent "interim statement of policy by the staff and governors" in the summer of 1980 opens with the ringing declaration:

> North Westminster is determined to be a school of excellence and declares itself to be a "learning school", a "family school", and a "community school" . . . the pupils of the school come from a rich and impressively diverse range of communities with different cultural backgrounds, ethnic origins, indigenous beliefs, occupations, social family patterns, economic positions and mother tongues. We are determined that the curriculum, the activities and the life of the school should actively reflect this richness, for we believe that the variety and cultural diversity of our pupils is an immense strength for us all.[15]

One programme objective which could bring about a considerable and relevant change in the curriculum content of those pupils who, in the earlier quotation, have been defined as possessing special education needs, was given as follows:

> We hope that local people and their activities will be brought into the school to inform, stimulate, guide and entertain the pupils and the work of local industries, trade unions, artistic groups, churches, and social organisations, will be displayed within the school to the pupils and that local writers, musicians, performers, speakers and others, will visit pupils and other audiences. Such a concern will necessarily involve going out into the community to observe, to study, to participate and to offer contributions (e.g., community services).

These examples have demonstrated the feasibility of schools which are non-authoritarian, caring about both pupils and staff, concerned for both the emotional and cognitive development of their pupils, outward-looking and involving a large number of adults so that the hidden curriculum imparts the notion that learning continues over the whole life-cycle. So far the discussion has not touched upon arrangements for meeting any special needs of particular groups.

Black pupils

Special efforts have to be made to build a strong relationship when there is a local black community. Boards of Governors, PTAs and other representative bodies should reflect the ethnic composition of the society. Black people should be encouraged to participate. A document from a Minority Group Support Service (MGSS)[16] urges that home–school links should not be in one direction only. It suggests that teachers should be aware of the West Indian tradition of visiting schools only in emergencies and of expecting schools to educate their children without inter- ference from the home; black parents still trust teachers to take responsibility for their children's education and teachers unfortu- nately sometimes interpret this as lack of interest. Nevertheless, black parents ask for accurate information; they want an honest assessment of their children's performance, and they become disillusioned by well-intentioned glowing reports that do not reflect a pupil's true academic ability and potential examination results. Supplementary education can play a part in raising levels of achievement by providing workspace, guidance and moti- vation for homework sessions. There has been a considerable growth in this movement, which includes Saturday schools, church schools, study groups etc., and shows quite plainly that Caribbean parents are interested in and concerned about the education of their children. It also indicates a massive distrust of the state education system which only a strong community programme can hope to correct. This was strongly reflected in the MGSS document which cited racism as the major cause of under- achievement. Racism was defined as: "The feeling of innate superiority held by people of one race in relation to those of another race, and the hostile behaviour which may result."

"A society in which there exists vast inequalities of access to resources and power, uses differential experiences in childhood to perpetuate such inequalities." Whether this statement is accepted or not – and it is difficult to think of grounds for objection – the fact is that black people believe "our society uses ethnicity as one method of producing a powerless group". There are too few models of black success presented and too few black teachers. The total ethos of the school should reflect the presence of black people in British society – whether or not it has black pupils. There are mixed views about the adoption of a school policy on racism. After a copy of a National Front leaflet was found in one school in north London, the school drafted a policy with a number of specific proposals including a campaign of education in assemblies, in lessons and during form periods which should achieve the following:

1. a) Impress upon all pupils that discrimination against people because of colour of their skin or place of origin is wrong.
b) Explain that black people, Cypriots and Asians have a right to live in this country – combat myths about immigration.
c) Prevent racialist abuse inside school whenever possible. Terms like "coon", "nigger", "Paki", "wog" should not go unchallenged.
2. Use films, factsheets and stories positively.
3. Confiscate racialist literature. The National Front is qualitatively different from other political groups in that it is openly and proudly racialist.

Despite the ever-present risk that positive policies may be counter-productive by attracting attention to the very phenomena they wish to deplore, I would argue that schools should adopt such policies, and should be told to do so by their local authorities.

Provision for special educational needs

It can make no sense at all to embrace a community philosophy and then to adopt a segregationist approach to those with special needs. Whenever and wherever possible, I would argue, they must share all the curriculum experiences that a community school opens up.

It is my belief that basic studies units (or whatever the pseudonym adopted) will have the best chance of making an impact if the teachers seek to involve themselves as consultants, as well as providing a haven and specialist skilled teaching for those with learning difficulties. Smith (1982)[17] has suggested a possible consultant role in which a remedial teacher might help *colleagues* to cope, and this seems a most promising extension of the specialist teacher's work. The qualities required for the exercise of such a role, Smith suggested, are empathy, respect and warmth. The consultant should be seen as an expert, but equal in status to the person being assisted; and, above all, a good listener, one seen not to gloat over the difficulties being confided. The decisive quality is likely to be that the consultant knows something which will make a difference *now*.

A department containing "remedial" pupils described in Hegarty and Pocklington's *Case Studies in Integration*[18] seemed to meet few of these criteria. The "slow learner" department was a major department within the school, comprising a Unit for those with severe learning difficulties and special classes for those with moderate difficulties. It had its own head, a senior teacher, and two deputy heads, one of whom was responsible for the Unit. It enjoyed "a higher status in the school than is usual in such departments": it was administratively part of the school but had a high level of autonomy. Its operational aims could be considered at the departmental level or those of individual pupils. The main policy decision was to blur distinctions *within the department* between the range of learning difficulties catered for: moderate, severe, remedial. "The reality of some differences was not denied but efforts were made to play down their significance." Integration was mainly conceived in terms of staff teaching across the department as a whole rather than always remaining with a particular group of pupils – and even this degree of "integration" proved difficult to put into practice for many years.

It was a stated intention to seek active working links with the main school but "this has tended to proceed relatively cautiously, with the emphasis on careful planning and setting up channels of integration which can be pressed into use whenever appropriate". "Blanket" integration has been avoided; for members of this department, the process of integration has to be "a planned and prepared absorption which recognizes at once the need for separately taught skills . . . and the possibilities for social mixing and common learning within a structure which does not make impossible emotional demands on the children involved." The staff, in this account, saw little possibility of integrating pupils with severe learning difficulties. Those with moderate learning difficulties were placed in special classes and some of them might eventually be integrated into main school, following formal re-assessment by the head of department and his staff in consultation with an educational psychologist. (pp. 49–50).

It certainly looks, from this account, as if pupils like Eldridge, Anne and Lincoln, might be placed in such a department, where their peer contacts would be largely confined to "integrating" with others much more severely disabled than they were themselves. We have already seen that these pupils were resentful of being withdrawn for special attention. Finding the right balance between helping and harming is extremely difficult, and the unintended outcomes of well-meaning policies often outweigh the good work that is undoubtedly done in such departments.

I visited such a Unit in another comprehensive school. The staff had refurbished a stock-room for use as a staff room, rather than walk the twenty yards or so to the common-room (though the barriers might have been mental rather than physical!). Thus there was little interaction between the special educators and the subject teachers, which can only be regarded as a tragic loss of opportunity. It would be surprising if the other pupils had not come to regard those in the Unit as a species apart. The only pupils from the main school visiting the Unit were those labelled "remedial" and even though they might have been receiving skilled help, this was clearly not the correct place for them to be taught in. This was immediately recognized by a new head of department appointed shortly after my visit, who obtained rooms for remedial work in the main building and separate from the special Unit. But, of course, that further increased the isolation of the severely disabled!

The processes by which we label pupils may turn out to be more influential in causing learning difficulties than any other activity teachers engage in, and may completely undo the benefits of the skilled tuition which is offered. For this reason, I would argue against Disruptive Units sited off school premises. They have grown considerably in numbers; as long ago as 1980 Her Majesty's Inspectorate found nearly 250 Units with 6,000 pupils. Their rationale seems to be grounded in a social deprivation theory that supposes low levels of interest of parents, low literacy levels in the homes, low expectations and low aspirations and, when applied to ethnic minority groups, poor self-image as the result of discrimination and rejection by the dominant white group. While there is certainly some justification for these suppositions such "psychological" explanations may encourage a "treatment" approach intended to bring about behaviour which conforms to school norms, at a time when such norms are bound to be seen as less relevant because of youth unemployment. There is a danger that Disruptive Units may contain disproportionately large numbers from ethnic minority groups. Then there are the very serious limitations in the curriculum, the lack of examination courses, the difficulty of returning to the mainstream and the lack of defined status so that even when they do have management committees, these do not include parents, or community representatives. (Advisory Centre for Education[19]). The Advisory Centre's report particularly objects to the "treatment ethos" which seems to emphasize behaviour modification techniques. These are criticized on the grounds that they:

- say nothing about the content of education
- deny intrinsic rewards associated with learning, depending instead upon "systematic bribery"

- give more control to teachers
- offer token rewards, therefore token learning
- leave the system unquestioned.

This may be unfair to individual Units, but, on the whole, they do seem to be institutions whose existence is very difficult to justify. Whenever possible, treatment of behavioural difficulties should be undertaken within the normal school organization, and special units within schools can avoid all these criticisms through a properly planned programme of integrated activities. Totally unmanageable behaviour may require the provision of special help outside the normal school, but it should surely always be undertaken on the surmise that an improvement can be effected and that contact with the school should be maintained.

Similar worries about the effects of segregation *within* the school afflicted Ken Williams, head of a remedial department in a comprehensive school. He had built up a full network of remedial classes, one for each year group, but although it was a "successful" department, returning a good proportion of students to the mainstream and achieving good standards of literacy and numeracy, he felt the pupils were missing out on some essential social experiences. He observed, for instance, that one teacher was very possessive over her class and was unconsciously hindering their wider social development.

Because of the statutory size of class (20 pupils), each year 6–7 pupils were placed in a remedial class when they might have coped in another stream and their performance may well have been depressed. Also, in many ways, remedial classes for the older pupils were becoming "pools of maladjustment". Despite, then, an overall successful department, acknowledged as such by the rest of the school, Williams decided upon a reorganization: the entire intake was placed in only three ability bands. As a result he felt that there was much greater participation in social activities; 80 per cent of the pupils in the lowest band were actively engaged in at least one of the evening activities arranged after school and were accepted by the other pupils as full and equal members of their groups. Williams concluded:

> Both the schemes I have described have strengths and weaknesses.
> I prefer the school without an organization of remedial classes and have given some reasons for my choice. Neither scheme is perfect and some children have suffered under both and some individuals have benefited under both.[20]

A survey of articles in *Remedial Education* over the last five years reveals growing support for the practice of withdrawal groups, within-school retreat centres, or any form of provision which as far as possible retains the pupils within the mainstream:

> My experience in remedial teaching has led me to believe it is crucial for children with learning difficulty to have a classroom in the main building and not a hut on the campus. We are aiming to integrate our pupils into the mainstream so why draw attention to them by placing them in a hut away from the mainstream? Eliz. Falconer Hall and Georgina Mitchell (Vol. 16, 1)[21]

> My experience as head of the remedial department in a boy's secondary school of 1,100 which operates both special classes and withdrawal sessions, shows that withdrawal is most valuable as an adjunct and a support to work in special classes or in regular English classes. Doris Kelly (Vol. 16, 2)[22]

While the greatest care has to be exercised in integrating special and remedial education (in part because special class pupils may be legally ascertained by procedures which occur mostly outside the school, and decisions regarding remedial pupils are generally those of the school itself) nevertheless there are examples of departments which have successfully negotiated the different roles and have succeeded in providing an adequate, safe harbour for those pupils requiring special care, while also managing to reach out into the school as a whole and to provide expertise for those whose difficulties are more within the normal range. Wilson & Broadhead[23] described one such example in which the aims of the special educational class were essentially the same as those for all secondary age pupils, but stated more specifically and in terms of learning behaviours. They were to:

- develop understanding and acceptance of their own distinguishing and disabling features;
- be sufficiently skilful to enable them to live as normally as possible in the community;
- have an adequate self-concept;
- be able to seek, secure, perform and retain a job.

In this school, remedial education was seen as a service available not only to pupils but also to subject teachers by members of the Guidance Department, who provided specialist teaching, particularly to remedy deficits in basic skills of literacy and numeracy through short-term, intensive involvement. Longer-term support was also provided, so that each pupil was working at maximum capability, and would still receive the full benefit of the school curriculum without being educationally handicapped because of the specific difficulties, while others learned slowly; differences in nature, cause, manifestation and treatment were noted and prevented any neat grouping arrangements. Pupils described as under-achieving came to remedial education only when the under-achievement had its roots in educational problems within the remit of the department.

Some examples of the short-term, intensive client-orientated, programmes provided by this Guidance Department may be helpful to others wishing to follow their pattern. They would provide supportive teaching in any of the following forms:

A single lesson for each of several weeks, spent on some aspect of a subject to allow the pupil to continue successfully with work in the regular class, where otherwise this small educational deficit could have hindered progress and confidence.

Helping over specific difficulty with one skill, e.g., poor spelling or note-taking in pupils who could otherwise pursue an academic course of study.

Teaching retarded skills with a whole subject area, such as mathematics – pupils were withdrawn from such classes and taught entirely by remedial teachers; attempts were made to return pupils every six months with improved number skills.

Treatment of retarded communication skills, usually shared with the English department – some pupils with very severe difficulty were withdrawn from classes to spend up to half their time each week on remedial work in communication skills, arithmetic and environmental studies. The other half of the week was spent on regular classes, again with support from and discussion between the teachers involved – and arrangements were made with their subject teachers to overcome the effects of segregation from their peer group.

This continuum of different abilities and needs extended to special class pupils too; a near-infinite variety was revealed; very able, backward, dull, learning disabled, under-achieving pupils; so that individualized educational programmes were the only practical response. Not all the work was undertaken in classrooms by the remedial specialists; many teachers throughout the school helped either directly ("on loan") or indirectly, by using individual and group methods. Thus the department was in no way separate from the rest of the school and pupils' learning difficulties were discussed with class, subject and guidance teachers, social workers, the school doctor and speech therapist, and parents.

Moving forward from remedial education

The above model is an excellent one for meeting special educational needs in large secondary schools. It is notable for a number of features:

★ The remedial department is an integral part of the school – yet has a clear identity.
★ There is constant exchange between department staff and all other school staff.
★ Specialist tutorial skills are abundantly available.
★ There is great flexibility of provision, including various forms of withdrawal and special classes as required.

Teachers in such departments tend to be community-minded in the sense that they expect to know and to involve parents whenever possible. They will be experimental and adventurous in their choice of learning materials and will be well equipped to cope with the challenges of a broader-based community school.

However, though a survey of twenty secondary remedial departments (Bailey)[24] provided an encouraging account of the activities and attitudes of these schools, it also revealed a lack of expertise in some important aspects; including a reluctance to:

1. Consider the use of parents and voluntary helpers.
2. Use pupil interviews, staff questionnaires and parental reports.
3. Involve themselves with remedial education after the third year.
4. Work alongside colleagues in the classroom.
5. Give advice to other colleagues on teaching handicapped pupils, reading development in other subject areas, preparation of curriculum materials and other techniques for use in the ordinary classroom.

Now these five activities seem to me to cover almost all the requirements for creating a learning environment for special educational needs in the coming two decades; and it appears that the specialist skills available fall well short of what is required. Remedial education, when applied with the sophistication of the above quoted models, certainly provides an excellent springboard; but the skilled teachers who can help those who are ready to leap are not being trained under present conditions. It was considerations like these which led Manchester Education Authority to disband its well-organized remedial advisory service and to create in its place a *Language Literacy and Numeracy Support Service* with the much wider brief of supporting teachers in the classroom. The Support Service began with a year's re-orientation course and has gradually evolved its own systems, resources and techniques, growing to more than sixty teachers in the process. There is a case for developing teams within comprehensive schools in much the same way, tackling different aspects of curriculum development as they evolve. Alderman Callow School and Community College have, in fact, set up a "support service" which, as well as operating a "haven" and a well-equipped remedial resources area, offers help on other curriculum matters. It prepares, among other useful material, "support guidelines", one of which, on "producing worksheets", gives excellent advice on readability, writing and design, production, presentation of worksheets to pupils and evaluation.

But yet more is required, and it is for those who know about special educational needs to become actively involved in curriculum negotiations. Dyson[25] reveals a wordly-wise attitude in an article entitled: "It's not what you do, it's the way that you do it." He found that the rational model of change provided in texts was about as much use as a street map to someone on the Underground. Curriculum change is a political business and his way round the problem was "to open up my concerns to anyone who would listen". He set up a working party to consider the curriculum of low attainers, invited everyone and made the point that innovation was always a joint venture, thus offering the ordinary teachers an opportunity to influence decisions in the school, perhaps for the first time in their careers.

Dyson's working party found that the problem was not simply that what was being taught was inappropriate but that the structure of the school and curriculum actually imposed that inappropriateness on teacher and pupil alike. "If you ask someone to teach something called Geography to a group of pupils with special needs for an hour or so a week over two years, the chances are you will get a watered-down version of what the teacher learned as geography at college." To stop this happening, the curriculum has to provide enough flexibility for teachers to teach what they want and for pupils to learn what they want. Two-year courses had to go, it was decided, along with assumptions about studying a subject in depth. In a final act of sophistication, this working party abolished itself before the curriculum it had established began to be taught, "so as not to be unduly influential in its application".

What was achieved, according to Dyson's account, was that:

In a hierarchical, fragmented high school, it is now possible to consider what is taught to the less able without reference to traditional subject areas; there is a means for biologist to talk to woodworker and mathematician to historian . . . the teacher can now think of teaching what he would like to teach and for the length of time he would like to teach it. . . . Moreover, he has a means of influencing high-level decisions which affect what he teaches . . . the pupils have a way of choosing what they learn and hence of influencing what they are taught.

Changes have been effected at Dyson's George Stephenson High School and a way forward from "remedial teaching" has been pioneered. Teachers with interests in special educational needs can learn from this experience that they have to become actively involved in breaking down the static curriculum . . . they have to look at how decisions about their pupils are made in the school, at least as much as at what those decisions are; and they have to find some way of improving their position at the bottom of the hierarchy so that they can play a dynamic role in curriculum decision-making.

Specialist teachers who wish to become effective in this area of school activity must have clearly articulated ideas about methods of teaching and about curriculum content, so that they know what to fight for. Faced with an entirely new population, they have in effect to create a new pedagogy. Existing systems are either irrelevant to this age group, or have been shown not to work very effectively.

Improving methods of teaching

Fortunately, some principles which could guide course development for these pupils can be derived from the practical experience of teachers in good schools, such as some of those cited above, in colleges of further education and in schemes organized under the auspices of the Manpower Services Commission.

Detailed illustrations of the way in which these principles can be implemented within the curriculum are given in Chapter 4, but it will be worth while to pick out three essential prerequisites from Figure 2.5 for immediate discussion. Pupils cannot learn effectively if they have a poor view of themselves as learners, are not actively involved in the learning process or are unable to read prescribed texts.

---

*Figure 2.5   Some principles underlying effective courses for
low-attaining pupils*

1. The courses should be relevant to real-life as perceived by these pupils.
2. The courses should be of short duration, with a definite end-product in mind.
3. They should be so organized as to enhance the status of the student.
4. They should involve the learner actively, avoid passivity and, wherever possible, provide the opportunity of acquiring a new skill.
5. The wide range of special educational needs should be noted and accommodated by an equally varied set of methods.
6. Team work as well as individualized learning should be incorporated.
7. The reading demands and the writing demands of curriculum materials should be reduced and supplemented by additional aids to literacy.
8. All courses should provide ample opportunities for discussion and oral work.

Enhance the status of the student

Many texts on secondary schools still refer to "children" and this sets an unfortunate tone. They should be called pupils or students-terms which have a more adult ring. Despite the size and complexity of community colleges and comprehensive schools, the pupils have to be organized in such a way as to indicate that they are regarded as worthwhile people. The models established throughout the organizational structures of the school are among the most potent determinants of pupil behaviour; it is the capacity to create a positive, caring atmosphere which so distinguishes the best special schools, and the opposite capacity which marks the worst of the inner city comprehensive schools.

There is the question of what to expect – not too much, but definitely not too little; with skilful guidance most pupils do better, and some astoundingly so. Various forms of self-assessment have been used to increase the involvement of the learner in a task and to enable him or her to achieve a realistic profile of abilities and disabilities. There are many systems available[26] which can serve as models but they seem too complicated and time consuming for normal school use. Basically all that is required is some form of report which invites critical self-appraisal in terms of on-task behaviour, skills acquired and the pupil's intentions for future usages. The aim is to encourage the pupils to reflect on their own performance as learners. This has been a major feature of the reading materials developed by Science Research Associates, and the self-marking and self-recording elements have always been very popular with the pupils in my experience. If properly introduced by the teacher they have had none of the deleterious effects associated with "cheating", chiefly, I suspect, because copying answers to not-very-difficult questions is even more boring than answering not-very-difficult questions.

Appraisals of pupils' performance by members of staff can also be very productive, provided sufficient time is allowed for proper discussion, and there is no procedure more likely to convince the pupils that they are accepted as people, even though the subject matter may be rather painful. Conversations based upon simple assessment forms completed by members of staff and the pupil have been recorded by the Industrial Training Research Unit (ITRU).[27] Statements indicating two extremes of opinion were found to be sufficient to enable pupils to structure their thoughts. (Figure 2.6)

Another way to raise the status of pupils is to invite their views on the content of the courses they are being asked to take. This need not be as radical a procedure as it sounds, but there is no doubt that an opportunity to take part in such discussions may lead to some comment about what is generally taught. Pupils comment on their courses anyway – but usually nobody listens.

The questionnaire in Figure 2.7, prepared by the Health Education Council,[28] has been used by many schools to enable pupils to participate in choosing topics they would like included in their courses. The range of choice is limited by the available resources, human and material, but it is still quite wide. A parallel form has been prepared for parents and this represents an interesting extension of the principle of consultation, which does not seem to have produced any upheavals, and is, in fact, quite commonplace. Perhaps other subject areas could usefully follow this example. The lower the attainment, the *more* important it is to convince pupils that their opinions matter.

Involve the learner actively

As regards *what* is taught, the most obvious way to kill interest is to avoid "controversial" topics. On the other hand, introducing

Figure 2.6   Periodic assessment: sample response by trainee

INTERESTED 1. IN OTHERS	to know more about other people so that I can be	SELF-INTERESTED
WANTS TO 2. LEARN	I want to learn new ideas do different things	RELUCTANT TO TRY NEW IDEAS
3. IS TOLERANT	I find it hard to answer this question	IS INTOLERANT
HAS HOPES FOR 4. THE FUTURE	I want to be doing something that I enjoy and life for the future, something that I'm doing now	NO INTEREST IN FUTURE
IS WILLING 5. TO DISCUSS	I'm not willing to discuss I don't talk much	UNWILLING TO DISCUSS
SHOWS 6. CONFIDENCE	I haven't got much confidence to do or make a move. I'm not sure sometimes I have a little bit of confidence.	LACKS CONFIDENCE
SHOWS 7. INITIATIVE	Sometimes I need people to show me the way.	NEEDS DIRECTION
ACCEPTED 8. EASILY BY OTHERS	I don't get on well with people. I never have been accepted quite as quickly as other people.	NOT EASILY ACCEPTED BY OTHERS

Source: I.T.R.U., Cambridge[27]

such issues into the classroom requires careful preparation, strong nerves and a properly conceived strategy.

The most conspicuous example cited in the present book is the issue of unemployment. Among older pupils, there seems to me to be no case at all for avoiding discussion of this, or indeed of most embarrassing questions, if this is what the group really wants to talk about. However, the direct way is not necessarily the only or the best, and some techniques are available to enable

Figure 2.7   Health topic questionnaire for pupils

m		f	
male			female age class/form

Listed below are twenty-eight topics to do with health. We want to know which of these topics you think are important to learn about in school. Please think about each topic and then put a tick in the box to show if your interest is HIGH, MEDIUM, LOW or NIL. If you tick the HIGH BOX, then you are very interested in that topic and would like to see it covered in school. MEDIUM means that you are interested, but don't think that it's so important to cover it. LOW means you are not very interested but wouldn't mind covering it, and NIL means that you don't want to cover that topic.

When you have finished choose the three topics that you think are the most important. Write the numbers of these topics in the 1st, 2nd and 3rd choice boxes opposite. *Thank you for your cooperation.*

1ST CHOICE	2ND CHOICE	3RD CHOICE

TOPIC	INTEREST LEVEL (tick one box for each topic)			
	HIGH	MEDIUM	LOW	NIL
1. Health services (doctors, dentists, hospitals, etc.)	☐	☐	☐	☐
2. Safety in the home	☐	☐	☐	☐
3. Drinking alcohol	☐	☐	☐	☐
4. Handicapped people	☐	☐	☐	☐
5. Sex	☐	☐	☐	☐
6. Conservation (protecting trees, animals, etc.)	☐	☐	☐	☐
7. First Aid	☐	☐	☐	☐
8. Nutrition (how food affects your health)	☐	☐	☐	☐
9. Venereal disease (VD)	☐	☐	☐	☐
10. Control of body weight	☐	☐	☐	☐
11. Cancer	☐	☐	☐	☐
12. Using leisure time	☐	☐	☐	☐
13. Road safety	☐	☐	☐	☐
14. Water safety	☐	☐	☐	☐
15. Growth and development (of a young person becoming an adult)	☐	☐	☐	☐
16. Morality (the difference between right and wrong)	☐	☐	☐	☐
17. Personal hygiene	☐	☐	☐	☐
18. Care of very young children	☐	☐	☐	☐
19. Personal relationships (getting on with other people)	☐	☐	☐	☐
20. Taking drugs	☐	☐	☐	☐
21. Contraception (birth control)	☐	☐	☐	☐
22. Exercise and health	☐	☐	☐	☐
23. Smoking	☐	☐	☐	☐
24. Mental health (health of the mind)	☐	☐	☐	☐
25. Pollution	☐	☐	☐	☐
26. The internal organs of the human body (and how they work)	☐	☐	☐	☐
27. Dental health	☐	☐	☐	☐
28. Common diseases that can be caught from other people	☐	☐	☐	☐

the teacher to avoid possible confrontations by adopting other roles.

The role of *neutral chairman* was advocated by Lawrence Stenhouse, Director of the Humanities Curriculum Project, whose basis, aims, procedures and techniques were outlined in a pamphlet *The Humanities Curriculum Project; An Introduction*.[29] The methodology was worked out through a collation of discussion materials, comprising both print and non-print materials. In printed form there were poems and songs, extracts from drama, novels and biography, letters, reports and articles, maps, cartoons, questionnaires, graphs and tables. Non-print material consisted of taped material – folk songs, interviews, poems, extracts from plays – films and slides. All this was assembled in packs under eight themes: education, war and society, relationships between the sexes, the family people and work, living in cities, poverty and law and order. Over this past decade the material has naturally dated but the idea of such collections has caught on, and they are usually available in comprehensive schools and often from Teachers' Centres.

The responsibilities of a chairman were identified as:

1. setting a context favourable to discussion
2. encouraging group identity and group loyalty
3. fostering in the group a commitment to the inquiry
4. ensuring a clear articulation of the subject under discussion
5. keeping under scrutiny the relevance of the contributions to the discussion
6. protecting divergence of view
7. introducing appropriate evidence
8. maintaining continuity between discussions
9. seeing that the rules of discussion which have been accepted are observed
10. mediating critical standards which support work of quality in the group
11. ensuring that an inquiry is rounded off in a way which organizes the understanding gained.

The handbook lists the main types of useful contribution made by a chairman prior to the discussions:

1. asking questions or posing problems in relation to resources

2. clarifying or asking a member to clarify what has been said as a basis for discussion
3. summarizing the main trends in the discussion
4. keeping the discussion relevant and progressive
5. helping members of the group to use and build on each other's ideas
6. helping the group to raise and define issues for discussion and to decide on priorities
7. questioning, providing intellectual stimulus and encouraging self-criticism.

One very important result of the experience of the development schools is the "Self-Training Procedure for Teachers" included in the handbook, with an important checklist of points to bear in mind when playing back and analysing tapes of discussions. The handbook also contains notes on activities other than discussion, such as assessment, notes for planners and annotated transcripts of audio-taped classroom discussions in extract.

Within this framework, discussion of controversial issues requires some drawing back of the teacher's normal authority and some approximation to neutrality. It is perhaps impartiality rather than neutrality which is desirable,[30] and from time to time – say when racial abuse is used, or overheard – a strong expression of personal disapproval would seem to be essential. But the semi-circular group, under an impartial chairman, provides an excellent opportunity for frank, orderly and systematic discussion of adult issues, and an essential opportunity for training older pupils to contribute in a slightly formal, disciplined manner which will be useful to them in other situations.

The successful use of this approach must depend upon previous experience of oral language work, discussion and consideration of social issues at a simpler level. *Lifeline*[31] (the Moral Education Curriculum Project) has an underlying methodology which is rarely used but it is worth making the effort to read the teacher's manual.

Discussions or verbal expression about observation and experience is important in virtually all areas of the curriculum. Oral work also reduces some of the pressures on literacy skills, and though it may be difficult for teachers at any level to accept that to express an idea verbally is as important as to write it down, this message must be accepted in the electronic age. Even now, tape recorders are not as widely used as might be expected, but they should be universally available for all pupils with special needs.

A particularly happy example concerned the case of Audrey

and Beverley, two third-year girls, second-generation Jamaicans who came into English class one morning very anxious to talk about something (Richmond, 1982):[32]

> I gave them a tape-recorder and they went out on the landing, saying that the discussion was about inflation. During the next half-hour, whenever I approached the door leading to the staircase, they waved me away through the glass panels. Eventually Audrey came into the room and said that I could go and listen to the tape if I liked. When I got there, both she and Beverley had disappeared, and I listened to the tape by myself. It is about race and racial prejudice, the Notting Hill carnival, slavery, South Africa, Rhodesia, unemployment.

The transcript makes fascinating reading and is reported with the care and honesty which characterizes *The Vauxhall Papers*. Very fluent, logically coherent dialogue was recorded. Richmond took the opportunity to ask the girls to write about the same subject and was able to compare the written and spoken versions. Since "in the mythology of the school", Audrey is judged "bright" and Beverley "less able", this was an exceptional opportunity. "A read of the transcript of their discussion makes it clear that such judgements are preposterous and that . . . the linear conceptions of intelligence by which most teachers understand their children are inadequate to the reality."

In Richmond's view the reason for Beverley's lower status was that she showed less technical control of the norms of written standard English than her friend. There is much to ponder here and the raw material would not be there but for the tape recorder.

Imaginative teachers can sustain this degree of involvement in any area of the curriculum. These comments on the use of Nuffield Science were from a science adviser who had seen the teaching of his subject to pupils with special needs transformed:

> I have to hand the comments of four teachers, two of whom are dealing with the Secondary Science Project (13 to 16 age group) and two with the Combined Science project (11 to 13 age group). Individual opinions will, of course, be coloured by personal teaching attitudes and ability. It must also be stressed that my sample has had to be very limited since few of the schools involved in Nuffield work have distinct ability streams. The replies are from teachers who take sets of backward children. In general it would appear that both projects are successful with the bottom 20 per cent. Reasons given are their relevance to life, and that they are pupil-based in outlook, and sufficient apparatus has been made available to make investigations interesting. In all cases much adaptation of the materials has been necessary involving leaving

out difficult concepts, avoiding mathematics where possible, producing simple worksheets and using direct teaching if it has been found that "circus" arrangements are too confusing.

Also what comes out is that the teachers have been surprised by the degree of interest in topics which previously they might have thought too difficult. The students have risen to the occasion to the best of their ability. Undoubtedly, some of the Nuffield Secondary Science materials will be significant for the least able pupils and there is plenty of evidence that both projects will prove progressively helpful across the whole 11 to 16 age and ability bands.

Reduce the reading demands of curriculum materials

The first technique available is, again, the tape recorder. Any printed material can be pre-recorded and heard, whether in the laboratory, home economics room, workshop or classroom, through a junction box and earphones. Preparing these cassettes provides an ideal task for parent and other volunteers, and older pupils will usually be willing to help in this way. It is so obvious, so simple, so cheap and readily available, that one can only ask: why it is not done universally? Twenty-odd years ago, the Wolverhampton Remedial Service had five hundred tapes in circulation, mostly used in conjunction with home-made concrete junction boxes and plastic earphones which worked very well.

It would be even more sensible if texts could be prepared which took into account some of the well-attested factors affecting readability.

When motivation to read is low, differences in readability have a considerable effect upon comprehension. Teachers would do well, therefore, to familiarize themselves with some of the features which influence readability, so as to select the texts which are the most accessible. Many pupils find schoolbooks boring in the extreme, like David, who said: "The work's O.K. I can stick at it. It's just the reading. The books are boring."

Lunzer and Gardner (1979)[32] asked 12 and 15-year-olds (N = 200) to judge passages from various subject areas from schoolbooks. The 12-year-olds rated six out of twenty-four passages as being very or fairly interesting while the 15-year-olds gave the same rating to only one out of sixteen passages. Whether or not these attitudes would be found among all pupils, they point to a considerable degree of dissatisfaction with the content and presentation of texts. The elements identified in Figure 2.8 can be helpful in deciding which to adopt and even a quick inspection

---

Figure 2.8   Some factors affecting readability

1. LEGIBILITY
   Size of print
   inter-linear spacing
   margins – line length
   type face
   illustrations and colour

2. ORGANIZATION
   use of bold type, underlining or italicizing
   logic and sequencing
   use of overviews, summaries, diagrams

3. VOCABULARY AND CONCEPTUAL DIFFICULTY
   vocabulary (measured by word length and word frequency)
   conceptual difficulty
   – complexity of the ideas
   – idea density

4. SYNTAX
   for example, the following aid readability:
   – active rather than passive verb
   – active verb rather than abstract noun formed from the
     verb
   – few clauses per sentence

5. INTEREST LEVEL
   appropriate to age group, sex

---

based on such a framework can provide a reasonably accurate estimate of readability.

This is not the place to enter into a discussion of readability formulae, but one of them is so easy to use that it is worth recommending to those teachers who have not met it before: this is the FRY GRAPH. It has limitations in common with other formulae in that it does not take account of any aspects of legibility other than sentence length and number of syllables. Those who wish to pursue the question of assessing readability will find an excellent source in Harrison (1980).[34]

"Cloze procedure" is a most valuable and under used method of assessing readability, which has the added advantage of direct contact with pupils. The term was first used by Wilson Taylor in

1953 to describe a new way of testing comprehension by deleting words in a passage on a regular basis, say every fifth word. The number of correctly guessed words is used as an indication of how much the reader has understood. Fifth and seventh word deletions are most commonly used. More frequent deletion than every fifth word leaves insufficient contextual information for the reader to work out the meaning; less frequent than every seventh word produces a sampled extract so long that the additional information has very little effect upon the score.

Cloze procedure has four uses:

1. readability measurement;
2. standardized comprehension testing;
3. diagnosis of individual readers' abilities or deficiencies;
4. reading development.

As a readability measurement, cloze tests are prepared on a number of passages and the same group of pupils are asked to complete them. The mean percentage of correctly predicted words is used as an index of difficulty. These percentages can be compared, with the lowest percentage indicating the hardest passage and the highest percentage indicating the easiest.

The notion of 75 per cent and 90 per cent correct answers in comprehension tests has proved useful, and the terms *instructional* and *independent* level have been attached to these percentages. Pupils achieving 75 per cent correct answers are at the instructional level – they can gain enough from it to be able to use the text when a teacher is available. To be able to work independently, a much higher percentage of correct responses has to be achieved.

These techniques create awareness of the pupils' difficulties and point the way towards better, more accessible texts. It is an area of reading development which has been neglected, compared with remedial reading. Comparatively little attention has been paid to procedures which would help poor readers to participate in general curriculum work and the outlook for the poor reader who is interested in science, history or geography, remains bleak. Some curriculum projects have attempted to overcome this by using a wide range of resources – discussion sheets, slides, newspaper extracts, photographs, maps, statistics. Even when the reading demands of particular materials is high, pupils can be helped by careful selection and by using pictorial items, tapes or newspaper and magazine articles collected by the pupils themselves.

In science much depends on work cards and worksheets

prepared by teachers, but a survey of schools using Nuffield Science materials (Guilliford and Widlake)[35] revealed a considerable difference of opinion about the importance of worksheets. Teachers in a Staffordshire school thought that worksheets of any kind were contrary to the Nuffield spirit, but those in a Worcestershire school, on the other hand, thought the whole success of the approach depended upon the provision of duplicated material and wanted extra clerical help for this purpose. On the whole, those teachers who had studied the performance of their disadvantaged pupils, and tried to produce worksheets which relied as much as possible on non-verbal cueing and open-ended questions, seemed most successful.

Even in simplified work sheets it is difficult to avoid words which present difficulty to poor readers. Thus, we have "crystals", "vapour", "condensed", "liquid", "parallel", "circuit", "series" – words which are unlikely to have been met in remedial reading books. Some of these words would not yield easily to attempts to "sound" them out, even if the pupil had acquired some phonic skills. Drawing attention to these words, getting the pupils to list them and to learn them in remedial reading sessions would help and some "technical" words would be suitable for learning through the making of a science picture-dictionary.

Although pupils with special needs may enjoy and learn from their science lessons, they may be defeated by traditional examinations. They cannot cope with the handwriting required; they cannot organize their knowledge quickly and coherently enough, and often they cannot read the questions or grasp their significance. One school has attempted to overcome the examination problem in an interesting way. The same paper was set for the whole year group and they were graded right across the year, but the remedial class answered their paper orally. The science teacher took them into the language laboratory and explained in detail what was required; then each question was put to the pupils orally and their answers were recorded. The tapes disproved any idea that these were non-verbal people Many of the answers were thoroughly adequate and yet, if they had been required to write them, they would have received an 'E' grade. Naturally, few reached the top 25 percentile but the teacher pointed out that many of them had scored 'C', a grade which would have been completely beyond their capabilities had it been a written examination. Thus they were able to compare grades with the top streams and some of them were obtaining marks equivalent to those of the more able, which was obviously very good for their morale. The teacher was not of the opinion that the

'A' stream would have raised their grades proportionately had *they* been allowed to record, because the difference between written and oral attainment in their case was less dramatic.

A most sophisticated account of oral testing in science was given over a decade ago in *Schools Council Examinations Bulletin 21 – C.S.E: an Experiment in the Oral Examining of Chemistry* (Evans/ Methuen Educational, 1971). This investigation found that the oral examination had "a reasonably high reliability and a reasonably high validity" and was interesting and potentially valuable. It was felt that an oral examination could serve as an instrument of external moderation and as a satisfactory method of assessment for those schools choosing the Mode II or Mode III forms of examination. But nothing much has happened in the intervening decade.

It is not really possible to divorce method from curriculum content, and many of these questions of method will be raised again in Chapter 4. However, the above suggestions may have served to disperse any despondency which might have been induced by the preceding analysis of the enormous problems facing schools. New methods do make considerable demands on both pupils and teachers and an adjustment period is inevitable. For example, in discussion groups pupils may initially remain silent, not because they have nothing to say but because the topics are unfamiliar, the situation strange. However, many schools have reported that, following an adjustment period, those with special needs are even more willing to contribute orally than the rest of their peers.

In general, it is quite clear that methods can be, and have been, devised to help older pupils with special needs and it is encouraging that these have been validated under a variety of classroom conditions.

References

1. HOLT, John (1969) *How Children Fail*, Penguin; (1969) *The Underachieving School*, Penguin; (1982) *Teach Your Own*, Penguin.
2. RUTTER, M. (1981) "Secondary school practice and pupil success", in MARLAND, M. *Education for the Inner City*, Heinemann.
3. Experimental World Literacy Project (1973) UNESCO.
4. FREIRE, P. (1972) *Pedagogy of the Oppressed*, Penguin.
5. BRITISH BROADCASTING CORPORATION (1978) *Parents and School*.

6. CUMMINGS, C.E. (1981) *Making the Change. A Study of the Process of the Abolition of Corporal Punishment,* Scottish Council for Research in Education.
7. MASLOW, A.H. (1970) *Motivation and Personality,* Harper and Row.
8. RUTTER, M. *et al* (1980) *15000 Hours,* Open Books.
9. Material from Widlake, P. and Piper, M. in MARLAND, M. (Ed.) *op. cit.*
10. REE, H. (1973) *Educator Extraordinary: A Biography of Henry Morris,* Longman.
11. *Network* Monthly newspaper of the Community Education Development Centre, Briton Road, Coventry. Also: "Going community" pack.
12. *Network* (as above).
13. *Network* (as above).
14. Craigroyston Community School: Interim Report from the Van Leer Foundation.
15. MARLAND, M. (1982) "North Westminster community school" *J. Community Educ.* 1,3.
16. Minority Group Support Service (1982) *Enabling Black Children to Fulfil their Potential,* Southfield, Coventry.
17. SMITH, C.J. (1982) "Helping colleagues cope – A consultant role for the remedial teacher", *Remedial Education* 17,2.
18. HEGARTY, R.S. and POCKLINGTON, K. (1982) *Integration in Action Case Studies in the Integration of Pupils with Special Needs,* NFER/Nelson.
19. Advisory Centre for Education (1981) *Report on Disruptive Units.*
20. WILLIAMS, K. (1977) "The role of the remedial department in a comprehensive school" in WIDLAKE, P. (ed) *Remedial Education: Programmes and Progress,* Longman/NARE.
21. HALL, E.F. and MITCHELL, G. (1981) "Provision for ESN(M) pupils in and eight form entry comprehensive school", *Remedial Education* 16,1.
22. KELLY, D. (1981) "Withdrawal for remedial help in secondary school", *Remedial Education* 16,2.
23. WILSON, J.M. and BROADHEAD, G. (1979) "Integrating special and remedial education in a Scottish Secondary School", *Remedial Education* 14,2.
24. BAILEY, T.J. (1981) "The secondary remedial teacher's role re-defined", *Remedial Education* 16,3.
25. DYSON, A. (1981) "It's not what you do – it's the way that you do it: Setting up a curriculum for less able high school pupils", *Remedial Education* 16,3.
26. For example, SWALES, T. (1979) *Record of Personal Achievement. An independent evolution of The Swindon RPA Scheme,* Schools Council.
27. Industrial Training Research Unit (1981) *Trainee Centred Reviewing on Youth Opportunity Programmes,* Cambridge.
28. The Health Education Council, 78 New Oxford Street, London WC1A 1AH.

29. *Humanities Curriculum Project: an introduction* (1970) The Schools Council/Nuffield Foundation, Heinemann Educational.
30. STENHOUSE, Laurence (1980) *Curriculum Research and Development in Action*, Heinemann Educational Books.
31. *Lifeline Moral Education Curriculum Project*, Longman.
32. RICHMOND, John (1982) *Becoming our own experts. The Vauxhall Papers.* I.L.E.A. English Centre, Sutherland Street, London SW1.
33. LUNZER, E. and GARDNER, K. (1979) *The Effective Use of Reading*, Heinemann Educational for the Schools Council.
34. HARRISON, C. (1980) *Readability in the Classroom*, Cambridge University Press.
35. GULLIFORD, R. and WIDLAKE, P. (1975) *Curriculum Materials for Disadvantaged Pupils*, Schools Council Curriculum Bulletin 5.

CHAPTER 3

Finding Out About the Hard to Teach

The teacher's task, the unique contribution he or she makes within a multidisciplinary team incorporating experts from other disciplines, para-professionals and interested lay people, is to encourage the pupil to start – or start again – on the road to learning. All the diagnostic procedures favoured by "learning difficulty" specialists are supposed to have this one aim: of producing an educational programme appropriate to the pupil's special needs. Here lies the teacher's professional responsibility and all too often, the specialist is unable to deliver. It is exceedingly simple to build up an immense file of information about the pupil's "problems" – poor intellectual capacity, lowly attainments in basic skills, inadequate home background. But what does it all add up to? What information do we have that can be used under normal school conditions, which usually preclude one-to-one relationships but quite often provide for small groups?

My experience of providing teachers with detailed statements about their pupils is considerable, and it does not encourage me to believe that this is the way to help produce high quality learning programmes. The information is simply not internalized by teachers because it is not communicated in a form which is appropriate. Only assessments in which the teachers themselves participate are, in my view, worth the time and trouble and to be effective they should lead immediately to suggestions for teaching, with a minimal gap between analysis and action. The analysis should concentrate on learning difficulties and the findings should be stated in terms which have meaning to teachers within a school setting. This does not imply a lack of sophistication but it probably does mean a rejection of many of the procedures which are at present utilized and their replacement by others which pay much more attention to how the pupils learn and how they might learn in the future rather than to what they have already learned. This represents a shift from a product to a process model which is reflected in the recently available work of Feuerstein and in other procedures developed by psychologists and sociologists who are most interested in "hearing the pupil's voice".[1]

Though this might sound obvious and though almost all teachers might want to claim that they know their pupils through and through, the facts are rather different. It is extremely hard to make contact with adolescents. Assessing and analysing the sources of their difficulties is not a simple task; responding to their observed needs in the last quarter of the twentieth century will require a response from teaching staff which at present can be observed in only a few schools.

It is not predominantly through the adoption of various "instruments" that increments in understanding will be achieved; the key to that door is already held by teachers. All they have to do is to turn it, open the door and listen to the flow of information from the people who enter. Since this proposition will sound improbable to many teachers, I will begin by quoting from one of the hundreds of case studies I have supervised on in-service courses for experienced teachers.[2]

Case study: Michael, a truant

A great deal can be done by studying a particular pupil and that pupil's problems at school, by evaluating the school's policies towards that pupil and one's own part in that policy. One teacher who carried out such a "case study" found the exercise very rewarding:

> Such a work re-aligns one's values so to speak, brings one back to the more solid ground upon which good teaching is practised; it modifies teacher's own behaviour with their pupils, it re-focuses the importance of their professional training. . . . Now I can say with honesty that my priorities at the beginning of the study were out of focus – that always the benefit of the child is paramount. In theory of course, I've always known this but one puts up a good case for "impedimenta" – I would with confidence and conviction say to an experienced "newcomer" to a case study that the interest engendered from the effort of involvement is ample recompense for the tedium of the initial stages. That is, in the re-sighting of

such seeming "trivia" as is brought about by a case study, it is possible to smelt together two fascinating treasures of experience – human development and one's own involvement therein.

In the case of Michael, a truant, the "usual" procedures had been followed – a warning on the first occasion and strapping on the second – but they had no effect. When the occasion came to cane the boy the teacher felt himself "unable to physically or in any other way punish him". Little was known of the boy's background except that he had a brother and sister and a father who had separated from his mother about four years previously. The mother was said to be a decent, hard-working woman who endeavoured to rear her children to the best of her ability. She had agreed to let her son stay with his father if it would help him to adjust and return to school – this was tried and abandoned within two weeks because of difficulties which had arisen between father and son.

These basic observations were supplemented by a visit to Michael's former primary school, where it transpired that he had been very happy. In order to elicit further information from the boy himself, the teacher had to make use of techniques which were new to his repertoire. The most important was no more than to encourage the pupil to talk about his situation, and for the teacher really to listen. Thus it emerged that the main reason for Michael's truanting was his fear of school and particularly of the deputy head responsible for discipline (the author of the case study)! This teacher undertook heroic modifications of his own behaviour, with some success. It became apparent that the boy was emotionally disturbed over his absent father, and by changing his policy towards Michael, the teacher brought the period of truancy to an end and greatly improved Michael's involvement in school life.

Now, though all this may seem simplistic and even banal to a psychologist, the point that can be missed by such critics is that a change in teacher behaviour actually occurred. Better relationships were established, and an improved regime was created for Michael. The case study that actively involves the teacher does bring about a reconsideration of values and a shift in behaviour which is rarely achieved by the more sophisticated methods advocated by educational psychologists. It is not that these are unusable – far from it, as is shown later in this chapter; it is more a matter of priorities. By far the most useful method of deriving information about pupils, now and in the future, is and will be the observations of teachers.

Using teachers' own observations and assessments

Almost all school decisions are based upon the rough-and-ready methods of recording information devised by busy teachers, frequently working under pressure. Often this information flow is entirely verbal and draws upon hazy memories and inaccurate perceptions. If school staffs could improve the quality of their observations about pupils, the results could be enormously beneficial, producing major reassessments not only of the pupil's position but also of the teacher's. If, as happens in many schools, the range of observations can be extended to incorporate contact with parents – especially in their homes – the increase in tolerance and understanding can be sufficient to alter the learning situation quite radically.

At the Sutton Centre in Nottinghamshire all the homes of first-year pupils are visited by a tutor who is allocated a group of about twenty-four with whom to keep contact, and this contact is maintained throughout the pupils' school life. The flow of information is continuous and discussions occur daily. They are mostly informal but occasionally occur in a more formal setting, as during a one-day in-service course and seminar (based in part upon an analysis of teachers' questionnaires by the present writer) which offered an opportunity for a review of policies to which the whole staff contributed. For the moment it may suffice to note the openness and capacity for self-assessment displayed by this staff, which (for me) constitutes the essential condition for constructive change.

Examples of the successful use of this technique are not confined to relatively "peaceful" areas of the country. The Parent Support Programme established in Liverpool included two schools in the Toxteth area. The scheme was designed to involve the local community, including parents, in the affairs of the school and for the school to offer a community facility. Each school had been provided with accommodation suitable for use by parents and a Teacher Key Worker and an Outreach Worker (mainly off site) had been appointed to each of the seventeen schools participating. A very good range of programmes had been developed and all reports on the work were highly favourable. It is ironic that the second phase of this parent programme – which was to have included the school which experienced a riot – was abandoned in the "cuts". Priority was given to improving the physical environment, a policy instigated by the Minister after the riots and his subsequent visit! It can only be surmised, but it would seem very likely, that had parents been present on the site and involved (as elsewhere in the scheme) the school riot might not have taken place.

I am arguing that, in assessing special educational needs, the most important element is not the preparation of suitable "instruments" – questionnaires, self-evaluation schedules, tests of ability and attainment and so on; it is the establishment of social situations in which all kinds of knowledge about pupils naturally becomes available, without fuss or strain, without Machiavellian strategems. Many schools have these kinds of arrangements and the results are clearly beneficial but some schools seem to be dominated by a belief that any show of empathy by the staff towards the pupils will cause a breakdown in discipline. A teacher in such an atmosphere who engages in conversation with a boy or girl, intending to elicit the pupil's feelings, is really doing something rather remarkable. It is likely to prove very difficult to encourage the pupil to talk much at all – which is one explanation for the "non-verbal" label attributed to "deprived" pupils by some influential writers in the sixties. They will not talk because – sensibly enough in the circumstances – they fear that what they say may be taken down and used in evidence against them. With perseverance, as in Michael's case, it is possible for a teacher with a sympathetic approach – even a newly discovered one – to gain the pupil's trust and a basic understanding of the problem. There is no doubt that this process can be greatly facilitated by the use of some simple instruments and techniques but these do require a certain amount of training before they can be used and interpreted successfully. Some of the more effective derive from Kelly's *Personal Construct Theory*[3] and have been applied to school situations by Ravenette[4]. One of his techniques is called "The Elaboration of Complaints". (Figure 3.1) Any teacher who can achieve a relationship in which the pupil will talk reasonably freely in a one-to-one situation may find it worth while to explore this technique. Those who would like to find out more might ask the Schools Psychological Service to provide a short training course.

The trouble with most psychological testing (to bring the chickens home to roost!) is that more and more data are generated but only a small part can be used by teachers in the treatment of the pupil's learning difficulties. The techniques described here can, of course, be abused but generally what pupils have to say about themselves and those in some way related to them has applications to each case. It needs drawing together and one way of doing this is to ask a number of teachers who know the particular pupil to complete some form of schedule.

Figure 3.1   The elaboration of complaints

The focus of this technique is quite simply the complaints which an individual voices against people who might be important in his/her life.
    The pattern of the enquiry runs:

1. The trouble with most . . . . . is . . . .
2. They are like that because . . . .
3. Another reason they are like that is . . . .
4. It would be better if . . . .
5. What difference would that make . . . . ?
6. What difference would that make to you?

(The people presented in (1) include boys, girls, teachers, brothers, sisters, fathers, mothers and self.)
    Start by reminding the pupils interviewed of the way a teacher might say "The trouble with that boy is . . ." or a mother might say "The trouble with that family is . . ." It is important to ensure that the complaint is the pupil's own and not an echo of an adult complaint. Denial of having any trouble is acceptable and in some ways as informative as an answer.

Example: "The trouble with most BROTHERS is the old brothers and sisters like to put the young ones down. They are like that because there might be some disagreement. It would be better if they stuck together and tried to work together. If this happened as they worked together they would really understand each other's feelings and if they understood my feelings they might be able to help me."

Johnson and her colleagues derived headings from the "symptoms of disaffection" identified by teachers in six schools. These demonstrated the great variety of pupil difficulties which worried teachers, and gave some idea of why teachers found them troublesome. (Figure 3.2)

I suggest that a case conference should be based on this schedule, completed by as many staff as possible. Since it is unlikely that the meeting could last more than about twenty minutes, a preliminary analysis of the completed schedules should be undertaken by whoever agrees to chair the session. Tentative proposals for a course of action can be derived from the recommendations but no attempt should be made to forestall the collective decisions. The more widely the chairing function circulates among the staff, the better.

Figure 3.2   A structure for describing "disruptive pupils"

Rate the pupils on a three-point scale (1 = low, 3 = high), using the description given after each item as deserving (3):

1. Attendance
    Unauthorized or persistent absence;
    persistent lateness for lessons
2. Attitudes to school work
    minimal work production
3. Behavioural deviations
    if (3) give description
4. Attitudes to school authority
    refusal to accept authority of teachers
    or selective in deciding which teachers
5. Personality abnormalities
    if (3) give description
6. Problems of communication
    impossible to "get through to"
7. Technical or intellectual inadequacy
8. Physical abnormalities or material
    deprivation
9. Social and family problems.

Linking analysis and treatment

I would argue strongly in favour of the clarification of purpose which can be achieved by defining "treatment" objectives, some of them in behavioural terms, but I dislike the behaviourist's assumption that these objectives can be imposed solely by the teacher. Such arrogance will not be permitted by adolescents and adults; in any case, the complexity of the learning process defies attempts to bring it within a simple paradigm. Whenever possible, pupils should be involved in the discussion that leads to the establishment of objectives and they should be kept actively involved through self-appraisal and self-correction.

The approaches illustrated in the next case study could certainly, given more time, have been refined and elaborated into something more systematic and sophisticated. Even so it was possible to identify the sources of the difficulties almost immediately and to evolve a method for resolving them – something which the schools and the "experts" had failed to do in ten years.

Case study: Derek, a well adjusted 15-year-old with a severe reading difficulty

Personal

Derek seemed a sensible, sensitive, polite adolescent boy, who talked confidently and was at ease with a "visiting teacher". He saw his strengths as in mathematics and football, and his inadequacies as reading and spelling. He felt it was his own fault that he could not read well. He had lacked motivation in his early school career and now felt it was too late, though he was still keen to learn. He appeared to lack confidence and was nervous of reading. His intelligence, when measured on an NFER test, was within the normal range.

His home background appeared to be supportive and caring. His mother was reported as being realistic about her son's ability and to want him to be happy in his future occupation. Derek had books at home, should he wish to spend his time reading, and the home was well provided in a material sense. Derek spoke warmly of his parents, brothers and sister and his home environment appeared to be stable, loving and secure.

Derek was a fit, healthy boy and his most recent medical examination showed no evidence of loss of hearing or poor eyesight. His speech was normal and he expressed his thoughts clearly and logically. He had lost no schooling through ill-health. Simple tests on the Neale Analysis of Reading Ability showed no impairment of visual or auditory discrimination.

School

He was looking forward to leaving school so that he could begin work as a painter and decorator, but he was concerned about his poor reading ability and revealed that he would like to read better. During a rather noisy lesson, when other boys were doing relatively little, Derek continued to work despite distractions around him. This did not make him unpopular in the group. Systematic efforts had been made by the school in an attempt to help Derek. He was given special lessons for the first three years on a one-to-one basis and in his final year was being taught in small groups. There did not appear to be one-to-one teaching at this stage. Derek reported that he liked his teachers and felt he could talk to them, while they for their part enjoyed teaching him, and indeed offered glowing reports that Derek was a sensible, mature, reliable boy and a conscientious worker.

Problem area

His difficulties in school were all focused on inadequate reading. On the NEALE Analysis of Reading Ability his accuracy score was 8.7 years and his comprehension age 9.5 years at a time when his chronological age was 15.9 years. He did not appear to have difficulty in visual perception because his ability to recognize letters and build words from their phonic constituents was about average. Nor was poor auditory perception a factor, because of his excellent comprehension and use of contextual clues. Poor short-term memory and poor self-image were also discounted.

The test "Get Reading Right" indicated areas of weakness as follows:

(i)   Letter sounds g,q,v,x,y,z. (Although he sounded "b" and "d" correctly on this first test, he later confused "b", "d" and "g").

(ii)   Final consonant blends: nk, it, Ip u-e, a-e, i-e, e-e.

(iii)   Initial consonant blends: pl, st, shr.

(iv)   Vowel digraphs: ew, oi, aw, er, ee, ur, oa, au, ai, or.

(v)   Consonant digraphs: ch, sh, gn.

(vi)   Silent letters: u, b, ugh, t.

(vii)   Word endings: ue, ion, cle, she, ge, tion, sion, ious, ed.

(viii) Multisyllabic words: most three, four and five syllabic words.

Treatment

Derek was due to leave school in a few weeks and so the adopted remediation programme had to be

(a) short but successful
(b) new, because all other methods seemed to have failed
(c) relevant to his needs and interests.

The overall aim was

(a) to improve Derek's confidence
(b) to improve reading fluency
(c) revive Derek's dying interest in reading.

Minimal Phonic Cues (MPC) is an aid devised for regularizing pronunciation which needs no expensive apparatus or books. The system is based on forty-five sounds and the pictures serve as a guide to the sound intended. Two symbols, the slur and the bar produce all the sounds needed, and unsounded letters have a cross above them. Where a symbol does not correspond with its spoken sound, the correct sound is put over the symbol. Therefore, if a pupil was asked to read:

x-
field, it would be marked field

x-   sx
science, it would be marked science

Pupils need only five minutes explanation before they can use this system. Looking at the MPC it became apparent that (i) Derek knew many of the given sounds, and (ii) the pictures were too childish, so an individual MPC was designed especially for him. The sounds shown on Derek's MPC were those of which he was unsure, and the pictures accompanying the sounds were photographs of famous footballers and teams. The system was introduced to Derek by explaining that it was a new method of teaching reading and one that he would enjoy and find easy. He was asked to give a few words, and they were written using the appropriate bars, slurs and crosses. "Together we looked at his MPC and he was immediately interested. We read the names of footballers and teams and each appropriate sound was pointed out."

Then he was given an article on football taken from an evening newspaper, which had previously been marked (Figure 3.3). After a few minutes he became accustomed to the system and read the entire article making only two errors which he corrected himself. Derek was obviously pleased on completing the exercise and when shown the original article he admitted that under normal circumstances he would not have attempted it. He was then asked to read the original article, which he did, making a few errors when the verb was printed in the past tense. The pronunciation rule about verbs ending in "t" was explained by showing him that "want*ed*" became "Ted", a boy's name. He liked the rule and offered more verbs ending in "t" so that he could practise this new skill. The first lesson was concluded by telling him that he had the ability to read well, but that practice was vital. "I felt sure that given a 'crash programme' his reading age could improve tremendously."

Derek's major weakness was vowel digraphs such as ou, ee, oa, au, ai, and certain consonant-vowel digraph blends such as ew, aw, er, r, ur. He had to be taught these, and learn to recognize them in words. At first these unknown sounds were "boxed" so that his attention would be immediately drawn to the focal point of the word, but this system did not work too successfully because the boxes detracted from the overall shape of the word, and probably served only to confuse the boy. Therefore the exercise was continued simply underlining the word and subsequently a different colour for the specific sound was used for immediate impact.

Before leaving the teacher gave him two new rules to learn. Because of his constant confusion between "b" and "d" a bed was drawn as seen below and its relevance explained.

(Taken from Frostig and Maslow (1973) p. 309)

He smiled and said he would try and remember. Secondly he was taught the difference between "knew" and "new" by pointing out that his name contained a "k" and he should therefore think that he "knows" the difference between the two words.

Remembering the original aim to start and complete all exercises successfully, Derek was given a short passage to read using the MPC system. He completed the exercise quickly.

The organization of the school timetable made individual tuition impossible, but there were many ways of ensuring that Derek continued to practise his reading in the classroom, and many of those ways were based around his interests. Collections of football cards were made, with which it was possible to play different card games. Competitive games were devised around "football strips" and writing was encouraged from games and comic strips found in the boys' magazines.

Techniques for analysing and treating reading difficulties along the same lines as those used with Derek are given in Figure 3.4 (pp. 68–9). In providing help towards the improvement of literacy skills of older pupils, the emphasis is best placed on enabling them to read a text of appropriate standard and interest as soon as possible. Any preliminary analysis that facilitates this process is worth considering; but essentially reading is about the getting of meaning from printed symbols for information and enjoyment.

Figure 3.3

Manchester United are flying in on two wings and a prayer for their F.A. Cup sixth round replay against Wolves at Molineux tonight. Tommy Docherty believes that luck will be the final deciding factor in this clash between two teams determined to reach the glittering semi-final with Derby County.

"If your name is on the cup, no one will beat you. How else could Bradford City win at Norwich and then lose at home to Southampton?" asked the Red's boss. So the Reds will tackle Wolves with a Wembley prayer this evening, but they won't be leaving it all to luck. "We have two wingers who could be key players for us at Molineux" said the Doc. "I don't see Wolves changing their style very much from the defensive way they played against us at Old Trafford. "They probably can't change, which is perhaps the reason why they are near the bottom of the table" said the United Manager. "Of course at the same time, they could always catch us on the bounce. But basically I believe it will be up to us to try and win the game."

Diagnostic assessment in secondary schools

The technique of diagnostic assessment has very wide applications in ordinary classroom teaching. It is "a means by which the teacher and pupil can find out what a pupil has or has not managed to learn and is, therefore, a guide to subsequent action".[5] Black and Dockrell concluded, on the basis of a long and thorough study, that three basic questions were being asked. "The teachers wanted to know how successful they were in teaching their class as a whole, which pupils were failing to attain the intended learning outcomes, and what were the reasons for each failure."

Now, there is nothing new in the notion that teachers should know what they expect their pupils to learn, and should take active measures to ascertain whether learning has occurred and should devise appropriate methods to ensure that those pupils who are failing should be offered alternative routes. The Scottish Council for Research in Education publication is very helpful, however, because it provides clear applications of these principles to recognizable school subjects such as geography and modern languages. An essential feature of such an approach is that the teacher has to clarify the aims and objectives of the learning programme as a whole and of the Unit within the programme.

There are immense potential benefits to both teachers and pupils in keeping a record of progress which so closely relates to the actual learning processes, and in completing it *during* the programme so that remedial measures can be provided immediately. A significant feature of such a progress chart is that it incorporates the pupil, who thus becomes actively involved in assessing his or her own performance. Successful teaching has as much in common with the arts as the sciences, and the capacity for sensitive interaction remains the key quality to be acquired. The use of a systematic recording system can, however, greatly facilitate the teacher's task and help to wed "the science of learning with the art of teaching".

The Schools Council has developed twelve programmes concerned with diagnostic assessment, learning and progress and pupil reporting[6] and these resources are readily available to teachers. However, in the long run, the more homely efforts of teachers working with the pupils they know well in their own schools are likely to have more enduring results.

References

1. JOHNSON, D. and others (1980) *Disaffected Pupils*, Educational Studies Unit, Brunel University. Subsequently (1982) *Schools and Disruptive Pupils*, Longman.
2. I wish to acknowledge with gratitude, permission to refer to this case study, and the subsequent one, from the teachers who wrote them while my students on an in-service course at Manchester Polytechnic. Derek's case has been published: LILLEY, S. (1977) *Derek: a case study*, *Remedial Education, Vol. 12 No. 1.*
3. For a short coherent account see COHEN, L. and MANION, L. (1980) *Research Methods in Education,* Croom Helm. Further Reading: BANNISTER, D. (ed. 1970) *Perspectives in Personal Construct Theory*, Academic Press.

4. RAVENETTE, A.T. "Psychological investigation of children and young people", in BANNISTER, D. (ed.) (1977) *New Perspectives in Personal Construct Theory*, Academic Press.
5. BLACK, H.D. and DOCKRELL, W.B. (1980) *Diagnostic Assessment in Secondary Schools*, Scottish Council for Research in Education.
6. COOPER, Don (1982) *Competence-based Education*, Schools Council.

Figure 3.4   Remediation of reading difficulties

Problem 1 Insufficient sight vocabulary

The pupil lacks the ability to group words into thought units which are necessary for comprehension and fluency. He/she is handicapped in attempting to identify new words by the use of context clues, because the vocabulary load of unknown words is too great. Possible causes:

1.   Lack of experiential background.
2.   Lack of incentive.
3.   Limited reading experience.
4.   Over use of alphabet and phonic methods in beginning instructions.
5.   Small speaking vocabulary.

Teaching suggestions

Various authors make innumerable suggestions for repairing insuffient sight vocabulary.

1.   Use oral impress method (pupil is trained to read in unison with teacher).
2.   Play games like "word bingo".
3.   Practice with flash cards/language master.
4.   Have pupils act out the words in groups.
5.   Practice with material designed for school computer.
6.   Use word box (keep a record of errors for each pupil).
7.   Give some kinaesthetic instruction.
8.   Separate words in a sentence by using a coloured material.
9.   Use markers to isolate words and emphasize the word/background relationship.
10. Use multi-sensory activities – tracing, miming.
11. Stress word meaning.
12. Elephant game (Good Reading).
13. Flash Cards (Ladybird).
14. Heads and Tails game (E. J. Arnold).
15. Key words reading games box.
16. Key words self-teaching cards.

Problem 2 Inadequate visual analysis skills

The pupil should be able to separate words into parts that are going to be useful to him in recognizing the words. He/she must be flexible in this skill so that if he/she finds his method of dividing words is unsuitable then he/she can quickly reappraise the words and reanalyse them. He/she should select the largest useable elements.

Possible causes

1.   Faulty approach to word recognition such as letter by letter spelling or sounding.
2.   Limited knowledge of vowel sounds.
3.   Hurried inspection of unfamiliar words to point where middles are neglected.
4.   Neglect of or overdependence on context.
5.   Dependence on one technique or use of the most inefficient ones.

Teaching suggestions

1.   Use discovery technique with groups of words having the same prefix.
2.   Give a direct explanation to words requested by pupils in the course of their reading.
3.   Identify root words within words.
4.   List antonyms in words by using affixes.
5.   Build a list of words based on several root words.
6.   Match affixes and meanings.
7.   Rewriting sentences.
8.   Structural analysis – word endings, plurals, compounds, possessives, syllabication, using school's computer if available.

Problem 3 Inadequate auditory analysis skills

The pupil must be able to apply phonic analysis to both easy and difficult words. The purpose of these phonic skills is the recognition of unknown words in meaningful context.

Possible causes

1.   Lacks auditory acuity.
2.   Lack of phonics training.
3.   Not ready for phonics training.
4.   Deficiencies in instruction – learns sounds of letters and memorizes rules without being shown how to apply them.

Teaching suggestions
1. Before using blends in reading, the teacher should work with very simple sentences or even words.
2. Cards containing the blends and a picture of an object whose name contains the appropriate sound help to consolidate these sounds.
3. The pupil should do exercises which require him/her to join a consonant blend to one or more endings.
4. Picture of object shown without consonant blend; pupil fills in consonant blend.
5. Teach new phonic skills with word pupil knows orally.

Problem 4 Inability to use context clues

Possible causes
1. Lacks training in using clues.
2. Word by word reading: limited vocabulary.
3. Carelessness in word recognition.
4. Teachers do not make use of contextual instruction.
5. Mental immaturity.
6. Lack of experience.
7. Material too difficult.
8. Lack of motivation.
9. Lack of phonic ability.

Teaching suggestions
1. Develop habit of verifying conclusions reached through other word recognition techniques by criterion "Does this make sense?"
2. Develop habit of examining context, sentences, paragraphs or whole selection, for clues to recognition and meaning.
3. Develop ability to use typographical aids.
4. Develop ability to use language structure aids.
5. Develop ability to interpret figures of speech.
6. Develop ability to use pictorial representations.

Problem 5 Inefficient rates of reading

Pupils need practice and guidance to develop flexibility in their reading rates. Some reading tasks require slow careful reading, while other reading materials can be treated with a much faster process involving skimming and scanning for relevant information.

Possible causes
1. Defective vision.
2. Narrow perceptual span.
3. Improper eye movements.
4. Emotional instability.
5. Material uninteresting or too difficult.
6. Small sight vocabulary.
7. Difficulties in word recognition.
8. Over-analysis in word identification.
9. Insufficient use of context clues.
10. Lack of phrasing.
11. Vocalization.
12. Use of crutches such as pointer or finger.
13. Deficiency in word understanding and comprehension.

Teaching suggestions
1. Introduce new words in phrases.
2. Use material that is easy and avoids inane repetition and has a considerable amount of conversation.
3. New dramatic readings, tape recordings, dummy or live microphone readings.
4. Encourage re-reading of selection to locate expressive phrases.
5. Have pupil prepare material to read orally.
6. Rapid exposure techniques of phrases.
7. Exercises: multiple choice in which choices are given in phrases; rapidly finding phrases to answer specific questions; marking off thought units in answer to questions; drawing line from phrase to word with similar meaning; locating phrases on certain pages that appeal to different senses.
8. Practice reading with set for
   a) recording a sequence of events
   b) specific detail
   c) causes of an event
9. Give practice in recognizing phrases as units during brief exposure through:
   a) flash cards
   b) tachistoscope

CHAPTER 4

Learning Across the Curriculum

The case for change in secondary schools has been argued in every chapter of this book, and it is stated again here. Brennan[1] has provided some valuable data on the content of secondary school courses for slow learners. Using their own subjective but consistently applied criteria of "successful" work, he and his team rated programmes in 255 schools by subject. By far the most "successful" courses were those for school leavers in special schools; similar courses in secondary schools were also estimated as "successful" in 43 per cent of the sample – higher than in any other "subject". But these courses were chiefly orientated towards a world of work, which no longer exists for many pupils. Beyond this, most subjects were rated very poorly and it is worth quoting the entire table.

"Successful" work with slow learners by curricular area

	% of schools with "successful" courses
School leavers' courses	43
English	31
Parenthood courses	27
Environmental studies	25
Social service	22
Integrated studies	21
Craft	18
Home economics	17
Art	17
Mathematics	16
Science	16

Humanities	12
Social studies	11
Drama	10
Music	9
Physical education/ movement	9
Rural science	7
Geography	7
Religious education/ Moral education	4
French	0
History	0

This table reveals the preoccupations of those concerned with schooling this group of pupils and also indicates the extreme ineffectiveness of the programmes. My own experience when I was visiting schools in preparation for writing *Teaching Materials for Pupils with Learning Difficulties*[2] parallelled that of Brennan's team: it was virtually impossible to find any consistently effective teaching of these pupils in secondary schools outside remedial departments. Unproven materials were dealt out freely to teachers of these pupils: they were outside the examination system and so could be "experimented upon", but there was little consideration of whether or not the materials met pupil needs.

In general, the programmes offered by the schools are so half-hearted and so obviously irrelevant to any present or future aspect of the students' lives that a very high proportion of pupils are quite willing to be passive observers, if not active perpetrators, of any misdemeanours that seem likely to enliven the school day. This overwhelming sense of futility is what every teacher finds so difficult to combat; nevertheless, there is no doubt that interesting, relevant, worthwhile programmes *can* be devised. Here is a concrete example, from Bretton Wood Community school.[3]

The staff started with a very positive attitude: "One golden attribute remains within the community school, adaptability and taking advantage of what we have." The school assumed:

1.   Students would rather return to school than be on the dole.
2.   Conventional timetable arrangements would be restrictive or counter-productive.
3.   Short courses would best meet the students' needs.
4.   Such courses must be linked in some way with the needs of the local community.

"A group of colleagues came together to plan a cluster of pilot courses – the timetable was adjusted accordingly – we were under way." It all seems too easy, but perhaps everything depends upon generating an atmosphere in which it is possible for "a group of colleagues to come together" and to reach agreement on basic principles of course planning.

The courses were of six to eight weeks' duration and offered one or two sessions of approximately two hours each per week, covering subject matter which ranged from business skills to sailing, from motor vehicle maintenance to the third world. Students could take courses either as single units or as part of a more conventional 16+ pattern or blend a number of courses across the four day and evening community programme. It turned out that short courses *did* motivate both students and staff, while unproductive courses could change direction or (though this did not happen) simply cease.

Sometimes courses advanced "to a point beyond which we had not dared hope". One such was the "auto-care" group which started with students working on a vehicle maintenance course but then responding to a suddenly perceived practical need to wash dirty cars: a simple introduction to reprographic work for advertising purposes produced a once-a-week offer of a cleaning service. Hard bargaining on price levels led to contract agreements, which included the cleaning of the school bus; "Bretton Auto-Care" was launched.

> The motivation to really get to grips with vehicle engineering; banking, involving the needs to solicit professional advice, and small business procedures; local advertising and quality control followed naturally and we now have one small independent working model of a cottage industry . . .

The enterprise and spirit shown by Bretton Wood is very typical of that which informs community schools generally, as their account went on to note:

> Spin-off effects are far-reaching and readily confirm a philosophy embodied within community education:
> (1) Adults and young people working and learning *together* is not abnormal; indeed, it is not merely accepted, but expected.
> (2) Ensuring that physical resources e.g. workshop, typing facilities, laboratories etc., are genuinely accessible leads to a more extended and mature use.
> (3) Spreading the time boundaries so that evening courses can become part of the full programme increases enormously the curriculum opportunities for everyone.

In the end it is a matter of basic commonsense put into effective practice – the removal of boundary attitudes makes it all possible.

Bretton Wood's enthusiasm and effective practice is by no means typical, as is quite clear from Brennan and Rutter, and the gap between the best and the worst schools is very wide. However, in this chapter I intend to report further upon practice which has produced good learning in a cheerful atmosphere, as opposed to little learning in a poisonous one. If anyone should suggest that the "less able" cannot take part in such learning experiences, I can only say that many of the reports are based upon sessions I have taught or observed myself with teachers and learners who were obviously enjoying themselves.

As the Warnock Report emphasizes, education should enlarge a pupil's knowledge, experience and imaginative understanding, and create an awareness of moral values and a capacity for enjoyment; it should enable pupils to become active, independent and responsible members of society.

In exploring current good practice, I have focused on three main areas:

1. The world of work, no work and increased leisure; and the "back-wash" effects this should have on schools.
2. The need for every pupil to have some grasp of the new technology which is coming to dominate our world, and enough mathematics and science to be able to understand what is happening.
3. More generally, the need to understand and make contact with the society of which school is a part, and to prepare pupils for it.

The world of work and no work

Mini Co-operative Companies

Mini Co-operative Companies are activities developed through the Clydebank/EEC Project.[4] They provide an experience of the working world somewhat similar to those available through the Work Experience on Employers' Premises (WEEP) provided by the Manpower Services Commission but differ from it in important respects – and also from work simulation exercises – because in a Mini Company pupils are actively responsible as directors, managers, shareholders, workers and salesforce in their own small-scale enterprise. They make and sell a real product and handle real money with which raw materials are bought and wages paid. They are enabled, through a species of action learning, to experience managerial, industrial, social and economic aspects of being at work. Moreover, the pupils have to learn to co-operate with others through a committee system and in the use of management structures, where they participate in decision-making which may affect the whole group. (Figure 4.1)

The experience in Clydebank suggests that it is perfectly feasible to set up a Mini Company within a school environment. Some may be a course lasting one term, one afternoon a week; but at least one Mini Company has slotted into the timetable with five periods (two double, one single) straddling business studies and the art room.

There can be no progress without the backing of the school, since the Mini Company is highly dependent upon the community for finance and sales. The young managers often receive support from their families and help and service from local industry and tradesmen. But, quite clearly, there must be powerful backing from within if the young people are to develop sufficient confidence to go out into the community seeking support. The Mini Company should be self-financing (through repayable share capital and sales of goods) to ensure there is no problem in budgeting; nevertheless it is essential for proper bookkeeping procedures to be followed, since the money to be handled might be quite considerable and must be accounted for.

The role of the teacher is vital. However, the Mini Company is a learning experience not a teaching situation and calls for a changed relationship. In the Clydebank project the terms used were:

★ initially, the adviser is an *animateur*
★ he/she becomes a process helper, if necessary, a *progress chaser*
★ finally, he/she might become a *resource person*, available when required, but no longer initiating the process.

Elizabeth Bray (1982), whose report is being followed here, feels that a Mini Company needs good products, which will be well within the young workers' capabilities and the school's facilities, and not too expensive in terms of labour and materials. She would prefer products of which the worker can be proud to those (for example, sweets bought wholesale) which can generate a rapid cash flow. One splendid idea is that the chosen product might be a model for students setting up a small business or workers' co-operative on leaving school. In fact, a high school in Edinburgh has actually been encouraging its pupils to set up one-

---

Figure 4.1 Mini Metals Company

Let us begin by eavesdropping on the final Shareholders' Meeting of Mini Metals (one of six miniature co-operative companies to which I have been an adviser). After three months in business, the "mini-co" Board were about to face their backers. The date: 16 December. Place: Clydebank.

The Managing Director, 15-year-old John, rose, glancing at his own shareholders – his father, an out of work shipyard scaffolder, and his mother, a hospital cleaner. Each had invested 60p in their son's enterprise. John shuffled his notes (from which I quote, with his permission):

> "Ladies and gentleman," he began, "I am the Managing Director of Mini Metals Company. I would like to begin by saying that the company was very successful and made a profit by your generosity (sic) on buying shares. Today is the Liquidation of the company and I would like to say I enjoyed it all very much. That is all I have to say."

John sat down amidst the applause of the shareholders – family, friends, teachers. It was the high point of his otherwise undistinguished school career. He then introduced a short slide show featuring each of Mini Metals' worker directors engaged in various tasks on the shop floor, in the boardroom, or at their desks as managers. With some help from the advisers, he outlined the responsibilities of the Board of Directors (the entire workforce were on the Board). We saw slides of John chairing meetings, with Jackie taking minutes. The Board, they explained, took the policy decisions – the choice of product, the election of the management team, and so on.

Next the Finance Manager gave an account of Mini Metals' finances. Share capital: £35. Turnover: £105. Outgoings included wages (25p per week to each worker), purchase of materials (iron strip, spray paint, flower pots), and overheads (the rent alone was 20p per week). The Production Manager then led the audience through the manufacture of their two products: their successful wrought iron holders for plants and their highly unprofitable line, metal wall plaques. All the directors took part in production, including the managers when they had completed their paperwork. Finally the Marketing Manager explained marketing as the key to success. All worker directors were also sales persons.

Finally, the Personnel Manager spoke. A spastic boy, he had made up for his low skills in production by his splendid sales record. "I would like to thank my associates and I would like to thank you, the people who are here today, for helping us to get this company off the ground."

Source: Elizabeth Bray, *The Clydebank Project*

man manufacturing businesses in their final year as a hedge against unemployment.

The project has similarities with, and differences from, a longer established version of the concept developed by Young Enterprise. Young Enterprise Companies are industry based, extra-curricular and specially tailored to the needs of older teenagers and sixth formers. They offer a special form of work experience which enables groups of about twenty young people – often a mixed-ability group and including, for example, sixth formers, junior management trainees and apprentices – to set up and run their own miniature company on the premises of a local firm. They meet one evening a week for about eight months; guided by advisers, they raise working capital, elect their own managers and manufacture their own product.

These ideas are usually confined to the more able pupils, but the Clydebank project and its forerunner in Shannon, Ireland, have been attempting to extend their applications to all pupils in secondary schools. They have developed the Mini Company concept, with back-up materials for younger and less able pupils, and have worked within the school environment and curriculum. In Shannon, Mini Companies were promoted within the curriculum by the SPIRALS project (Shannon Project of Intervention for Relevant Adolescent Learning) as a work simulation programme with participants ranging in age from 12 to 16. Some groups were of mixed ability but others consisted of lower ability and remedial pupils.

Work experience programmes

Clydebank, a town of about 56,000, has seen over 20,000 jobs disappear in the ten years prior to 1981, by which time over one in five of the working population was unemployed. Nevertheless, those pupils who were involved in work experience programmes were overwhelmingly in favour of them and external evaluation found that 93 per cent thought work experience would benefit all pupils in their last year of compulsory education. The students' reactions were very interesting. (Figure 4.2)

Even after the pupils had left school and were facing the realities of a world in which fewer than half would get jobs, 83 per cent still felt that work experience had been worth while. The practicalities of preparing for work experience were undertaken in the classroom. They included sending application forms to employers, making arrangements to reach the place of work and for meals, considering appropriate styles of dress; some briefing

---

**Figure 4.2 Work experience: responses of school
leavers in Clydebank**

%
96   It gave me an idea of what work is really like.
87   I enjoyed my Work Experience weeks.
81   Most of the time I was doing a real job.
79   I learned about a lot of different jobs.
65   The jobs I got were fairly easy.
62   I didn't want to go back to school after Work Experience.
61   You had to keep up with the work.
46   I found the jobs tiring.
44   I didn't learn about any jobs I'm interested in.
32   They just invented jobs to keep me busy.
19   I got the dirty jobs while the others had a rest.
15   I was bored most of the time.

---

was given on industrial safety and the pupils were encouraged to decide upon their own learning objectives.

Nowhere has a more thorough programme been implemented than by Coventry LEA which enabled over 1,500 pupils to take part in work preparation at local colleges of further education and TOPSHOP[5] between 1976–1980. Topshop, the Coventry Training workshops, has been established on two sites in the city, provided by local industry, and offers courses in catering, mechanics, clerical work, engineering, building, reprographics. These experiences were felt to be so successful that it was decided to develop work preparation programmes as an integral part of the careers and personal development programmes within the school's curriculum. A special unit to co-ordinate work preparation was set up and based at Topshop. The intention was to offer work preparation for all fourth and fifth year pupils and this was implemented in six secondary schools in 1981. The objectives of the programme of work preparation are stated in Figure 4.3.

Excellent log books have been prepared for pupils which contain model application forms, a checklist on personal matters, a short statement on the organizations of Topshop, and forms for individuals to complete – concerning personnel and locations, first impressions, the ways in which the experience was the same as school, how it was different, etc. There is a section on the language of industry, inviting the pupil to find out the meaning of terms such as management, shop steward, decision-making,

---

Figure 4.3 Objectives for work preparation programmes

1. To enable the pupil to experience the general needs of the world of work, both vocational and social.
2. To reinforce the school's personal development, careers and academic programmes by relating them directly to the work situation, thus increasing the pupil's motivation.
3. To enable the pupil to sample a type of work.
4. To increase the pupil's awareness of employer's requirements e.g.:

   reliability
   punctuality
   self-discipline
   interest and willingness to work.
5. To develop the pupil's understanding of company structure, role of management, trade unions and relationships at work.
6. To inform the pupil of further training and education opportunities which are available.
7. To demonstrate the practical importance of mathematical and communication skills.

---

disciplinary procedures. The pupils' attention is also called to Youth Opportunities Programmes so that they start thinking about future courses.

Technical and vocational educational initiative

An important initiative has recently been taken by the Secretary of State for Education: the introduction into schools of the *Technical and Vocational Educational Initiative,* funded not by the Department of Education and Science but by the Manpower Services Commission – the first time this organization has played a direct role in the development of school curriculum. It is a scheme for the 14–18 age group; it is in the nature of an experiment and varies across the fourteen LEAs which have been selected. It has definite commitments to the "less able" in that the school population is intended to cover the full range of ability. It offers a potential opportunity for specialists in learning difficulties to provide advice and supplementary materials. The objectives are "to widen and enrich the curriculum in a way which will help young people to prepare for the world of work and to develop skills and interests, including creative abilities, that will help them to a fuller life and to be able to contribute more to the life of the community".

TVEI, according to its public declarations, is not intended to bring about premature specialization, but rather, by providing a broad experience of work-related skills, to widen the understanding of this age group to the possibilities of "vocational education". In linking these two words, the originators of this scheme have cleverly moved on the debate about the respective contributions of "education" and "training", extending the definition of "vocational" to cover almost any school (or extra-school) subject, suggesting it is the nature of the programme which determines the term adopted to describe any particular course. Whatever the doubts about TVEI (and they are plentiful), it has been eagerly welcomed – and competed for – by LEAs and it has several effects: it identifies this age group as one particularly to be served by the education service; it identifies a particular kind of programme as a priority; and it suggests that existing practice is inadequate. For these and many other reasons, TVEI is well worth noting and its reports will be interesting reading. There seems little doubt that the precedent for curriculum development established for technical and vocational education can be followed in other areas of the curriculum; if so, the opportunities to contribute on behalf of the hard to teach should not be missed.

Schooling and unemployment

Whatever the role of TVEI or work experience in the curriculum, it is essential that schools should also recognize the structural changes occurring in our society which are likely to ensure that nearly all of the school leavers in the eighties and nineties will have some experience of being *without* work. What is perhaps most important is to convince young people that they need not be stigmatized by unemployment. Orwell noted: "what horrified me was to find that so many of them were ashamed of being unemployed". Mitchell (1982)[6] in a penetrating analysis of the effects of Youth Opportunity Programmes, suggested that every pupil of secondary school age (academically able or not) should at least be initiated into:

1. An up-to-date knowledge of the broad areas of employment nationally, manpower requirements in the future (as far as they can be detected) and current shifts – a knowledge of particular local conditions.

2. Survival skills – benefits, budgeting, psychological awareness
    of the problems of unemployment, adaptability – living in
    digs, sharing a flat, re-training, recognition of one's skills,
    especially removal of sex stereotyping in jobs.

3. Understanding of the causes of unemployment and potential
    solutions, the range of individual support services available,
    post-compulsory schooling including leisure services and
    opportunities.

Bindley & Parry (1981)[7] feel much more strongly. They describe
three courses given at the University of Manchester, which were
designed to help the unemployed. They say that despite implicit
criticism of the work ethic during the course, the students were
actually being prepared for re-absorption into a world of work
which no longer existed. They claim that it is not an educator's
task to deflect anger from its legitimate target, that is, the society
and the economic system that have caused this catastrophe. The
unemployed should be given an understanding of the economic,
political and social system in terms of its values and assumptions
in order to direct anger at those in line for blame – politicians,
treasury officials, multinational companies, etc. Is this merely
Utopian dreaming? Should education be concerned with the
"perceived needs" of the unemployed? But by whom are the
needs perceived? Surely very few unemployed would say they
need a course of this kind; the unemployed see themselves as
being in need of a job and this is exactly what the education
system cannot promise. It could be said that all education aimed
at the unemployed or potentially unemployed which is not
intended to give them a deeper understanding of the society in
which they live and the causes of their situation, and which does
not enable them to identify those responsible for their situation, is
merely a diversionary activity and palliative.

Fleming (1982)[8] who conducted a research project lasting two
years in three comprehensive schools in Sheffield, surveyed the
attitudes to school and work of low-attaining fifth-form leavers
during their last term at school and again one year later. She
investigated whether a young person's attitudes were related to
the degree of difficulty experienced in finding a first job after
leaving school and explored pupils' perceptions of the careers
activities they experienced in school. Two of her findings were:

1. These young people left school with attitudes very much in
    the mould of the work ethic, finding it very important
    personally to find a job, and seeing unemployment as a

"miserable" and "lonely" experience, entailing a deterioration in self-image. This was also what Lynne Whatley and Jeanne Armitage (1983)[15] discovered in their work with young unemployed females; these girls saw little purpose in YOP if it did not lead to jobs, and felt immensely let down at the end of their courses. Many of them fell into a state of withdrawal and depression, and remained indoors a great deal, spending as much time as possible in bed; others, reacting consciously or unconsciously to their situation, became mothers and found satisfaction in this role, no longer referring to unemployment. It would not appear to be a solution, at any level, except in the very short term since they were much less enthusiastic as the babies grew into toddlers and began to make heavier demands for time and attention.

2. During their last term at school, 44 per cent of pupils had not talked to *anyone* inside or outside of school about what it might be like if they could not get a job when they left school. Only 10 per cent reported having talked to teachers. Although heads of careers departments reported that their fifth form leavers were prepared for unemployment in terms of practicalities, 82 per cent of the pupils could not remember doing anything at school about unemployment: 45 per cent said they did not know where to go and claim social security and 81 per cent said they had not got any ideas from school as to how they might use their spare time if they were unemployed.

The following letter appeared in the *Daily Star*, 6 August 1982.

I am 16 years old and have just left school. I would like to know why, when we were at school, we were never taught about the big wide world! Why were we not told about tax, National Insurance, what Youth Opportunities are and how to sign on? But when we signed on for the first time we were expected to know where to go, what forms we needed and what we were entitled to.

Arising from these findings, and others which have shown that the vast majority of school leavers look for work within five miles of their homes, there are some fairly obvious but apparently rarely drawn conclusions. In general, school curricula must incorporate the notion of unemployment, however unpalatable it may seem. Fleming notes that it is usually presented in negative terms – "frustration of ambitions, lack of money and adult status, boredom, stigma and blame arise". Various responses are possible: one is certainly to ensure that the causes of unemployment are fully explored, that the structural nature of the shift in employment patterns is brought out and that feelings of personal inadequacy are diminished. Another is to prepare pupils specifically for life without employment but it is often difficult for anyone in an official position to recognize and act upon this.

At the National Elfrida Rathbone Association (NERA) Conference, July 1980, the Director, Dr Jim McKinnon, said ESN people must be trained for unemployment. This is already being done at NERA workshops where concentration is on life skills, not vocational skills. Dr McKinnon said he had applied for a grant from the MSC to develop this idea but they "Had a fit – they couldn't cope with the idea of preparing people for unemployment". Courses offered at NERA workshops to prepare people for unemployment include such simple things as cooking quick meals and looking after clothes.[9]

Leisure

Ten years ago, Fairbairn[10] considered the problem of rising unemployment and suggested measures which some still regard as new, such as job sharing, early retirement, less overtime and a shorter working week. Fairbairn cited one hundred American companies which had adopted the four-day week. But what is to be done with the extra leisure that will result from less work? Fairbairn stated that existing provision for evening classes was dull and inadequate and that the numbers availing themselves of existing provisions were falling. He called for greater effort to provide means by which people could put their extra leisure time to constructive use for self-improvement.

Even today, not everyone would agree with education for leisure; for example, an influential organization called YOUTH-AID[11] opposes it. At Youthaid's AGM in December 1980, Clare Short said that to speak of structural change in the economy which would make a return to full employment impossible was "confused, wrong and abhorrent". Nevertheless, if present trends continue, the beginning of 1984 will see only a small minority of 16–18-year-olds in work. Youthaid argued that this age group should be removed from the labour market and given further education and training. Those at a York Conference organized by the Centre for Study of Comprehensive Schools[12] called for a different emphasis; there should be a shorter working week, earlier retirement, less overtime and more job sharing but also people should be encouraged to think critically about the nature of work and the work ethic. It is not clear how schools can simultaneously fulfil this critical role and their traditional one as inculcators of good academic work habits and as the main agents for accreditation. Once again, we are in danger of throwing the burden of responsibility on to the shoulders of those who run the schools and who have no more claim to understand the complex mechanisms of society than anyone else. Nevertheless, whatever the future patterns of employment, it can be assumed that an important function of schools will be to orientate people not only towards paid work but also towards education as a potential source of satisfaction, and away from the notion of education as a service to be delivered. Schools will have to help pupils to perceive education as a process which rewards active partici-pation from its clients and can give satisfaction throughout life. There will be more disposable time available to people who until recently have had to work long hours; if used creatively, this becomes leisure time. The school has an obvious duty to intro-duce its pupils to the widest possible range of activities which are likely to be continued into future life.

One starting point is physical recreation. There was an interest-ing study (by Tungatt and Townsend, 1980)[13] of how people became involved in sports. Two areas of Stockton-on-Tees were sampled: 60 per cent of respondents were involved in or had been involved in some sport or other since leaving school, but only 23 per cent of these people said they had become involved at school in the sport they now practised. Yet they had been introduced to a wide variety of sports at school: soccer, swimming, tennis, badminton, table-tennis, cricket, netball, ten-pin bowling, ice-skating, motor cycling, canoeing and yoga. Most people were introduced to the sport in which they were now involved by friends and family – 50 per cent mentioned this source.

In another study, Pearson (1975)[14] revealed that there was a high level of non-participation in games at school and he attempted to clarify the situation. He found that non-participation was greatest in the lower ability bands, a particularly unfortunate state of affairs which calls for a revision of attitudes and policies on the part of those who organize physical activities in schools. Tungatt and Townsend found that pupils of both sexes and from all types of school were highly unlikely to cite any sport as their favourite curriculum activity and those who did so were pre-dominantly male and were usually those who excelled.

It certainly looks as if physical education teachers need to devise better methods of involving more pupils in activities which they enjoy and want to continue after leaving school. Exceptional facilities like Sutton Centre's ice-rink obviously cannot be repli-cated across the country, but much better use could be made of community facilities (for example, municipal golf courses) as is the practice with swimming baths. The Sports Council has made a big impact with its "Sport for All" campaign, and has recently funded *Action Sport*, a project in the West Midlands which makes maximum use of existing facilities to encourage unemployed people to participate in sport and recreation. When the right blend of opportunity and warmth of welcome is provided by the organizers, large numbers of people become interested and active. Probably the key to post-school participation is the formation at school of peer groups with a common interest. The *Unemployed Young Women* project[15] interviewed a large number who seemed bereft of interests and contacts, seeming not to have retained friendships made at school. "Commitment signifies that one's life has a meaning" (Hopson and Hough)[16] – but this is precisely what these young women lack. It seems obvious that they should be encouraged to maintain contacts through their schools. However, the clubs featured in school brochures (and reports from Youth and Community departments) somehow do not attract or retain a great many who would benefit from membership. Once again, it becomes abundantly clear that the establishment of administrative structures is only one small part of the task of providing an adequate service to those who need it most but are least likely to demand it.

Communications technology, science and mathematics

Virtually every week, a new communications system is announced, but the new technology seems to make little impact upon what most secondary schools do for most pupils with special needs. Curiously, the more severe the degree of handicap, the greater the degree of sophistication in provision. For example, Hegarty and Pocklington give an account of a specialist resource centre for primary age pupils with impaired vision located within an ordinary primary school (nursery to age 11). There were fourteen visually impaired pupils on roll. The resource area was purpose built comprising four rooms, two quite large and well equipped, and two others appropriate for small group work, including a pottery kiln which was also extensively used by main school pupils. "Given that they were all based in regular classes and used the resource area only for withdrawal work . . . the premises are highly satisfactory." Physical and material resources (which were intended to serve a number of schools in the area as well as this one) included an extensive range of low vision aids which anyone could try out (under the supervision of the peripatetic teacher); large print resources, a closed circuit television and a video-recorder and various large-scale play items.

There is rarely provision on a similar scale available to those with special needs in secondary schools. Learning difficulties of a moderate order do not attract so much sympathy and – what may be more important – remedies are not so readily apparent. Expensive apparatus is no guarantee of improved learning in pupils with moderate learning difficulties, whereas low vision aids bring immediate relief and benefit for those more severely disabled. Yet it is essential to offer the fresh opportunities provided by the new technology to all pupils with special needs.

Fortunately, video and sound cassettes, records and films, are generally available. All teachers are aware of these resources, but putting them to use is not always easy. There tend to be formidable organizational problems: competition among staff for apparatus and broadcasting time is the most obvious; more subtle, but potentially destructive, is the tendency for the broadcast material to degenerate into a series of *ad hoc* lessons, with little continuity or relationship to the normal school curriculum.

Radio

A recent innovation by BBC *Radio for Secondary Schools* can certainly help teachers in planning their courses. Night transmission means that schools with recording equipment and time switches can plan the use of programmes with much greater flexibility than previously, since whole series can be broadcast in a week. Teachers can then arrange to use the programmes in a way which suits them throughout the term. Sound radio is the most accessible of non-print resources and should be fully utilized, since listening skills are among the most important for pupils with literacy problems and "canned" programmes help teachers to enrich the curriculum experiences of the hard to teach. The quality and quantity of the programmes for schools is apparent in the catalogues issued by the broadcasting authorities. The BBC's 1983 programmes make a booklet 63 pages long and there are several series on special educational needs.

Television

Children during their primary school years spend an increasing amount of time watching television until it reaches about three to five hours daily by the age of 12. There is no consensus on whether this affects their learning in schools but studies reviewed by Gunter[17] definitely encourage the view that it does, in a number of ways. At a more superficial level, television may encourage "laziness" in regard to reading, which may also be reflected in reduced academic effort. At a deeper level, substantial periods spent in passive viewing may cause "interference and disruption during the formative stages of important creative, analytical and linguistic abilities". Reading is about meaning-getting, and requires – if progress is to be made beyond the earliest, mechanical stages – eager interaction between the reader and the text. Gunter concluded: "Difficult or illuminating passages may encourage the reader to draw upon his or her own experiences, memories or fantasies to add meaning to the written material. Most commercial television programmes however, essentially train children to sit passively and watch rather than to actively think and do."

During the 15,000 hours they spend in the compulsory school system, pupils who average three to five hours a day achieve 12–20,000 hours of television watching. That is to say, they spend at least as much time viewing as attending school, yet I have never heard of a movement to de-televise society!

There are controversies about the effects of television on children's behaviour but the arguments of those who dispute its impact appear to me less and less convincing. There seems little doubt that television, as the major source of entertainment and information for large sections of the population has a considerable influence on public opinion and beliefs. The Scarman report, which recorded many alleged instances of "copy-cat" rioting based on observation of the television coverage of the Brixton riots, emphasized:

> The need for newspaper editors, television and radio producers, and journalists to give continuous attention to the social implications of their awesome powers to influence the minds, the attitudes and the behaviour, not only of the reading, viewing and listening public, but also of those whose unlawful behaviour they report.

It does not follow, however, that the violent content of television programmes, as opposed, perhaps, to "news", is necessarily transferred by imitation into the young person's behaviour. It is unlikely that television is responsible for society's ills; as Gunter points out, if this were so, the numerous programmes containing examples of pro-social behaviour ought also to have an effect. "If its violent content actually does cause increases in social aggressiveness, can television, through its portrayal of altruistic behaviour, at the same time work to increase the general level of kindness in society?" He reaches the cheerful conclusion that it well might.

From this discussion, it follows that schools must take account of television, must make more use of its opportunities and must involve pupils in discussions of programmes. The videocassette age has already arrived and control of the content through forms of licensing and prosecutions is not likely to prove very effective, though few would dispute that the most vicious material should not be seen by children and young people. Secondary schools can play their part by making use of television's potential for producing positive social behaviour. They can attempt to exorcise its ill-effects through open-ended discussion developing "adolescent understanding, interest involvement, judgement and commitment, within the context of the world around them".

With the arrival of "Walkman" cassette tape recorders, teletext information services, breakfast television, cable television information services, and new computer-assisted learning materials, the school is losing its position as the sole or even the main place of learning. The eager and curious can learn anywhere; but secondary schools (compared with primary schools, or further education establishments), have a poor record in encouraging such eagerness and curiosity in those pupils who do not develop them at home.

Television and other forms of mass communication inevitably affect schools. A few schools have tried to seize the opportunity to provide specially-made learning aids for "slow learning pupils" but this is not sufficient. Schools will *have* to find ways to use television, videocassettes and other electronic aids, or risk being seen as obsolete. *Especially* with these pupils, adult-like content must be incorporated to supplement the patronizing and child-like fare which is often served up as being somehow appropriate to pupils of limited attainments. It is true that most LEAs have already accepted the potential of microcomputers, placing them in schools and ensuring that teachers undertake in-service courses to prepare for using them. However, the central question is how to exploit the new technology for the benefit of the hard to teach.

Making your own videos and films

Ways must be found to allow pupils (especially older ones) "hands-on" experience. In an amusement arcade it is possible to observe the compulsive attention that "Space Invader" machines command from youngsters who in school would be said to have an attention span of only a few seconds. Using a hand-held video camera can be equally engaging. I made a video film of children in a nursery school which achieved a considerable degree of success with parents. It was certainly a very bad film, made by the simple means of walking around and pointing the camera at anything which happened to interest me. However, one great advantage of these systems is that they produce excellent quality sound, so the children's conversation was easily audible, despite intrusive background noise. The parents were enthralled, pointing out their own children, commenting on the play and activities. A re-run was demanded. The children enjoyed it too.

A professional would have been horrified by the technical shortcomings, but the film fulfilled its limited purpose. There is plenty of fun to be had from film making and even quite crude material can be put to use if the audience is really interested in the subject matter of the film. A similar point of view was held by Cliff Parfit,[18] at that time head of a remedial department in a London comprehensive school, who made films with a "remedial" group of older pupils. He emphasized that the satisfaction of the whole group must come before the esoteric interests of the craft and that the criteria guiding film making at this level were quite different from those which might guide even a competent amateur. The student who becomes really interested in the techniques of film making can join a proper film club. In our context film making is used mainly as a tool.

Parfit's school had close contacts with several voluntary organizations and used the YMCA in particular as a base for outward looking activities; when invited to make a film, the YMCA agreed with alacrity. There was little time for preparation – "there never seems enough for all we want to do" – because the school had a tight schedule of day-to-day activities to maintain and only one afternoon could be given for the film. They followed up a suggestion from the West Indians in the group, that they interpret the "Blues" song "Nobody knows you when you're down and out". A rough outline was all that there was time for. The electricians were preparing the lights when the school party arrived at the studios. Rough props were put in position – a table and a few old chairs. The story concerned the trials of a girl living in a slum, who found lots of instant friends when she had a sudden windfall but who lost even the friends she had had previously when the money had gone. "The actors worked with remarkable intensity. Not too much emphasis was placed on getting every little detail correct. The need was merely to get the main outlines of the story firmly sketched." Then the film adviser arrived from the London Film Group. "One could not help but be impressed by the trusting manner in which he put expensive equipment into completely untrained hands." The film was shot very straight-forwardly and in sequence as if it were a play because in this way the actors were able to work creatively without much direction while preserving the story continuity. Breaks in the action were made for close-up shots and special effects – for example, fists being thrust into the camera in a fight sequence. Props were limited to an old pack of cards, a letter, some toy money and a bottle of ketchup. There was no time for boredom as everyone had a job to do, from moving the furniture and lights to fiddling with the record player and acting the bit parts. There was no time for endless attention to detail or many re-takes, only to get as much as possible in the "can" before the day was over. A few weeks later the group watched the first showing with "unalloyed pleasure" and quite extraordinary concentration!

Later ventures were more carefully prepared. One of the pupils produced a lavishly illustrated film script, depicting a young man who puts loyalty to a pop group before his affection for a self-centred girlfriend.

Parfit concluded that the film medium had many advantages in work with older pupils with special needs. It is *adult* even in the eyes of very sophisticated adolescents. It involves movement and activity without too much sitting at desks. There is a comprehensible and worthwhile end-product to the group's endeavours. Hard work and concentration count (and can be seen to count by these pupils). It provides a starting point and motivation for many kinds of creative and involving activity. It stimulates a critical impulse towards films and videos, which is extremely difficult to nurture in an age where "chewing-gum for the eyes"fills so much television screen time.

Microtechnology

Another experiment in "hands-on" learning has been developed by the Notting Dale Urban Studies Centre,[19] and has proved so successful that the government has put up a huge sum of money to start other similar centres all over the country. Although their work has been mainly with unemployed youth, the centre maintains links with primary and secondary schools and urges the need to use the city as a resource. Its main interest lies, however, in the Technology Centre where young people can learn about computing, microprocessors and electronics. This is based on ten years work done by London physics teachers and scientists from Imperial College. In this time they have developed a method of "doing science" with young people from unqualified backgrounds, often to a very high level of sophistication. The workshop/laboratories are based on this experience. The actual business of "penetrating" technology, according to this Centre, has to be founded on different learning notions from those used in traditional training.

Many so-called school failures are competent in electronic music or some other personal interest and the workshop extends beyond the formal hours of nine till five to tap and develop these interests. There are no set courses but the generous staff–trainee ratio allows "an opportunity to custom-build a framework for learning for each young person". This Centre, as has been remarked, has attracted considerable attention and I visited it with a party of teachers to find a most relaxed and welcoming group of young people. The atmosphere was right – it is not necessary to associate seriousness of purpose with solemnity. There seemed a lot here that could be applied to schools, especially the principles of offering instruction without too many preliminaries and of providing opportunities for young people to try out exciting technology.

Science

During visits I made while collecting material for a Schools Council report I observed many lessons where boys and girls with special needs were admitted to all the resources of the science laboratory, often using expensive apparatus with due care and attention. Especially exhilarating were classes where the teachers were enthusiasts for Nuffield Combined Science, where the experimental work is often designed as a "circus" in which the pupils, usually working in pairs, move freely from one situation to another. All pupils have the chance to become actively involved in science, to handle apparatus such as a circuit board and to explore it in their own way and at their own conceptual level.

In a Midlands 11–18 comprehensive school, there was a first-year group of boys and girls working on circuit-boards. These involve the use of a large number of easily losable bits and pieces but the pupils were working readily in pairs, spread out to all corners of a spacious laboratory. Although this arrangement afforded ample opportunities for time-wasting or damage, the pupils did not exploit them. It was, in fact, a most impressive class and the girls seemed to be enjoying it as much as the boys. The lesson was in two parts. In the first, the children were allowed to experiment with the boards, to set up and break the circuits as they chose. When this period seemed to be drawing to an end of its own accord, the remedial teacher issued worksheets with diagrams which had to be copied and a hypothesis to be tested, namely whether the bulb would light when a certain wiring arrangement was adopted. The recording was done simply through a yes/no worksheet. Most pupils had no difficulty in understanding how to record but when, on several occasions, they were not able to match the diagram and the circuit-board, the teacher helped them by orientating the circuit-boards (marking in the wires on the diagram in the same colour as the leads on the circuit-board) and talking them through it. In this way, all the children with difficulties resolved them and most of them completed the assignments. Most impressive was the hum of activity, the degree of involvement, the way in which pupils kept coming to the teacher and saying, "Look, it works: it lights", and the general feeling that they were happily and actively engaged in cognitive tasks which were a little bit ahead of their previous attainment.

However, a more recent investigation[20] into the state of science in schools has revealed some disturbing facts. In certain areas, there seems to be little knowledge of major science projects mounted by the Schools Council and the Nuffield Foundation. Incredible as it may seem, two remedial advisers working on a peripatetic basis in the North-East of England could not find any schools which were using these materials – and several had never heard of them at all. Worse, one school, in a local authority recently under close scrutiny for its level of educational spending, replied to our questionnaire:

> Regret no assistance is possible as none of the materials or packs which you mention have been seen, discussed or even heard of. Finance is such that we can barely cover stationery or replace common materials from capitation. Any project which may involve the purchase of fresh equipment/materials for any ability group is quite out of the question!

Science materials specifically intended for low attaining groups have recently become commercially available with the publication of *Open Science*.[21] There are thirteen pupils' units, a detailed teachers' guide and a set of record sheet masters.

Each of the 32-page pupils' units is clearly printed in black-and-white. The layout has been carefully designed with bold headings and clearly drawn diagrams. A reading level of approximately 10 years is assumed, and the material does not assume that pupils have previous scientific experience or knowledge of scientific concepts and principles. The activities in each of the units follow a similar format. Pupils are told which materials they will need, "What to do" and how to record their results. There are follow-up questions based on the activity. Units can be used either as consumable workbooks or as text books in combination with their science notebooks. Titles include: Fire, Safe Eating; Grow Your Own; Life Spotting; Structures; Snaps and Circuits; Electricity in the Home; Starting and Stopping; Keep Going; Pollution; Find Out about Machines; Machines on the Move; and Science at Home.

The teachers' guide gives practical advice on the classroom organization and teaching of each unit. Comprehensive lists and diagrams are also provided for the benefit of laboratory technicians. Teachers conducting the field trials felt that this project was particularly useful with pupils in the 14–16 age range but that it needed to be in the hands of experienced teachers. One school summarized the project materials as "no sinecure, but the rewards are worth the work".

Recent reports from the project's original headquarters show that more and more schools are adopting *Open Science* as a realistic approach to science for older, less academically motivated pupils. In the Birmingham area, a very successful Mode III CSE Course, based on the Project, has been adopted.

However, *Open Science* is just as effective in non-examination courses. One of the Project team's writers stressed that it complemented (rather than competed with) other science projects intended for this age group. For instance, teachers could design their own schemes using *Open Science at Work*[22] and LAMP (Less Academically Motivated Pupils) Project.[23]

Mathematics

When pupils in a maths lesson groan aloud, it may seem a fairly familiar reaction – sad, but typical of the way so many react, or have learned to react. These particular pupils, however, were complaining that the maths lesson was coming to an end. They did not want to finish, and go off and "play". These displays of involvement have been noted and recorded by teachers using Schools Council inspired learning materials: *Mathematics for the Majority*, and the *Kent Mathematics Project, Nuffield 5–11 Mathematics*. It is quite clear that approaches to learning mathematics exist which, if properly used by a skilled and enthusiastic teacher, easily overcome boredom and reluctance. Why, then, do so many pupils – and teachers – have such a mental block against mathematics, which seems to exceed anything to be found in other subjects?

Part of the difficulty lies in unresolved and apparently rather theoretical differences of opinion about what it is proper to teach. Those who are most influential in setting syllabuses tend to hold that it is mathematics in its "pure" form that really counts – they would place "the creative aspects of the subject and an awareness of its aesthetic appeal" very high on their list of priorities. In contrast, a group of teachers surveyed by Lumb[24] chose as their first aim the development of a positive attitude to mathematics as a valuable subject in which all children can gain some success and pleasure. These teachers were concerned with children in their middle years of schooling (9–13 age range) who experienced difficulty in the learning of mathematics. In turn, they differed from colleagues in many schools which have a tendency to give priority to the "quick recall of basic mathematics facts and to make this the main diet for remedial groups".

I brought together a group of teachers to discuss these different approaches.[20] Perhaps the most interesting aspect of our own early talk was a gradual acceptance that learning mathematics was much the same process as any other form of learning. Nuffield 5–11, the model given, served very well:

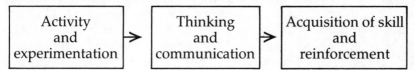

Activity and experimentation		Thinking and communication		Acquisition of skill and reinforcement

We would seem to have placed ourselves alongside those teachers who believe in making mathematics enjoyable; in developing an understanding through enquiry, experience and discovery; in making their pupils aware of the uses of mathematics beyond the classroom. All these aims were outlined in a DES document (*Mathematics 5–13: A Handbook of Suggestions*), but what has not been sufficiently emphasized is the intensity of the controversy about priorities within this broad consensus. The ideas of those who favour an emphasis on "life skills" – or even, as in *Mathematics for the Majority*, on the utilization of mathematics skills in other areas of the curriculum – are very far removed from those who set the tone for mathematics teaching.

The Cockcroft Report, *Mathematic Counts*,[25] places emphasis on the following points: that the different rates at which pupils learn

---

Figure 4.4 Is there a best policy for low attainers in mathematics?

There cannot be a single best policy because schools must take account of particular circumstances:

    expertise, attitudes and interests of staff
    needs of low attainers
    resources available

Successful policies are likely to:

1. take into account particular circumstances of schools
2. fit in with any existing overall school policy, in particular those relating to low attainers and to mathematics
3. be flexible enough to cater for the wide variations in pupils' needs
4. involve in their development all who will implement them
5. take account of available knowledge and resources relating to the teaching and learning of mathematics
6. be able to respond to changes in circumstances e.g. changes in staffing.

Source: Denvir B. *et al.* (1982)[26]

---

is a factor too often neglected; that much more attention should be given to practical work and applications. Above all, Cockroft firmly rejects the "back-to-basics" movement which (in the words of the Report) has encouraged some primary school teachers and some teachers of low attaining pupils in secondary schools to restrict their teaching largely to the acquisition of computational skills. A recently available source (Denvir *et al*, 1982)[26] calls attention to some ways of bringing about change. (Figure 4.4) Any approach will have limited success unless Denvir's point four is given due weight: we must involve in the development of policies all those who will implement them.

There have been some encouraging reports of successful teaching inspired by *Mathematics for the Majority* and the *Kent Mathematics Project* and Jean Roberts, a Birmingham teacher of the hard to teach, has even made successful use of the *Midlands Mathematics Experiment* which is generally regarded as being at too high a level for low attaining pupils:

What do I teach? Enjoyment, I hope! I try to widen their ideas, horizons, vocabulary, ability to discuss, reason, solve problems, suggest etc. especially as my classroom is an ex-cloakroom with windows high up in the walls and the view from the chairs is of brick walls and roofs! The school is designated social priority in an area of high unemployment and its allied problems.

Understanding and making contact with society

Social and moral education

Many of the curricular activities arising from issues of employment, unemployment, leisure, and science and society would be included in various schools under the heading of social education.

A coherent social education programme should seek to develop these skills in its pupils. In its widest sense social education should be promoted by every teacher of every subject. MacBeath and his team have provided a valuable starting-point. (Figure 4.5)

The Schools Council's *Moral Education Curriculum* project (led by Peter McPhail) capitalizes upon a broad analysis similar to that of MacBeath, but its materials are simpler and very successful in use. MEC regards social activities as having much in common with motor skills (such as cycling, skating, driving a car, playing the piano, typing, performing industrial tasks, playing tennis and other games) in that they are composed of skills which can be learned. If we accept this, it is possible to take a more optimistic view of the outcome of training in certain social skills.

McPhail hypothesized that adolescence is a period during which the number of "social experiments" made by an individual reaches a peak. He defined a "social experiment" as

> any situation when an individual exhibits a trial attitude or takes a trial course of action which calls forth and effects a reaction from any other individual or group of individuals, whether the attitude is adopted or action taken with a view to testing reaction, or with no conscious aim.

The "social experiment" in McPhail's view is a learning situation. A development of the argument is that the most fundamental kind of human learning is experimental or trial-and-error learning (even when this involves imitation). "The contention is that a sense of identity only follows the ability to predict the effects of one's actions and to modify one's environment." The adolescent asks "Who am I?" and this leads to other questions: "What can I cope with?" "Is my self-concept accepted by others?" "Is my social approach effective in terms of establishing the relationship I want?"

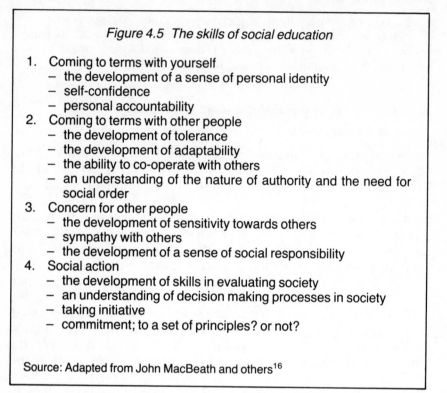

Figure 4.5 The skills of social education

1. Coming to terms with yourself
    − the development of a sense of personal identity
    − self-confidence
    − personal accountability
2. Coming to terms with other people
    − the development of tolerance
    − the development of adaptability
    − the ability to co-operate with others
    − an understanding of the nature of authority and the need for social order
3. Concern for other people
    − the development of sensitivity towards others
    − sympathy with others
    − the development of a sense of social responsibility
4. Social action
    − the development of skills in evaluating society
    − an understanding of decision making processes in society
    − taking initiative
    − commitment; to a set of principles? or not?

Source: Adapted from John MacBeath and others[16]

The Moral Education Curriculum Project rests upon sound theoretical foundations and McPhail's own theoretical expositions are admirably concise. Nevertheless, the project has adopted a very pragmatic approach. Its working answer to the question "What is moral education?" was that all education which helped children to adopt a considerate style of life, to have respect for others' feelings and interests as well as their own, was moral education. Doctrine was confined to the assertion that:

> A world in which people are treated with consideration for their feelings and interests is preferable to one in which this is not the case – a piece of assertiveness which seemed unlikely to cut us off from the followers of any of the great religions or from agnostic or atheistic humanists.

The Moral Education Curriculum Project has published varied materials to help class teachers under the series title *Lifeline* (Longman). They include suggestions for situations on which to base discussion and role-playing (Figure 4.6).

Figure 4.6 Suggestions for discussion and role-playing

1. You are very attracted to a girl/boy but she/he ignores you.
2. A boy or girl of your own age with whom you are friendly appears to be very upset for some reason unknown to you.
3. You suggest to a friend that you both go on the "big wheel" at a fair but your friend seems reluctant.
7. The person in the next desk to you sniffs continually.
8. Your parents brag about you to their friends in your presence.
12. Your father is critical of your hair and of your clothes.
14. Your mother herself adopts teenage fashions.
17. An adult is critical of your parents in their absence.
31. You lend a coat to your cousin. When the coat is returned there is a cigarette burn in the lapel.
38. A boy in your form thinks that it is amusing to let down your bicycle tyres.

Suggestions for classroom use:
(a) Read out or write on the board "a situation" for consideration.
(b) Ask the members of the form to write down on a piece of paper what they would do in this situation.
(c) Ask for suggested courses of action or collect the papers and choose one to start with.
(d) Invite a group of pupils who have made a similar response to role-play the situation, the response to it and what they think would happen subsequently. (If they are initially reluctant, invite volunteers or ask them to argue in support of their response and encourage a discussion.)
(e) Initiate form criticism of the response and any other aspects of the role-play.
(f) Continue by inviting the role-play and/or discussion of further responses suggested by the pupils only as long as interest is strongly maintained.
(g) Some summing up by the form and the teacher is in order, but an obvious and emphatic commitment to one response by the teacher during the early stages of this work is not to be encouraged. It is better to discuss the pros and cons of different courses of action and leave the pupils to make a final judgement.

"Language" and humanities

There are other approaches to social and moral education than those reviewed so far, and I will now discuss two which both fit more conventionally within the "normal" school curriculum and have received recent field trials (Widlake 1983).[20] *Language in Use* is cited for three reasons:

a. it might serve as a model for other groups thinking of trying out "new" approaches
b. it indicates the extent to which disciplines overlap, but illustrates the significance of the contribution of a particular discipline – in this case "English"
c. it seems an admirable example of curriculum development, providing a firm structure within which a teacher (or team) might work, while leaving plenty of scope for the personal development of lesson materials.

"A veritable Aladdin's cave – full of ideas" was how one teacher reported on *Language in Use* – yet surprisingly, the field trials drew attention to the fact that these materials were not usually considered among resources for use with pupils with learning difficulties. Few teachers in remedial departments in secondary schools had heard of it and none had used it before the trials.

Language in Use[27] by Peter Doughty, John Pearce and Geoffrey Thornton was developed as part of the Schools Council Project in Linguistics and Language Teaching. It is a *teacher* resource, suggesting activities which aim to develop awareness and abilities in spoken and written language.

The teacher's book is the core of the materials. It consists of a loose-leaf binder with 110 sheets, each forming a unit providing an outline for lessons, grouped into specific themes which explore particular aspects of language in use. The themes are drawn together under three broad divisions:

I   Language – its nature and function
II   Language and individual man
III Language and social man

The teachers who reported on *Language in Use* work mainly in inner city comprehensive schools, but also in other urban areas and in one rural school. They were mainly involved in teaching in remedial and "basic skills" departments, but heads of English departments, members of support services, etc. were also included. Many teachers thought the materials effective as they stand:

> This approach is seen as *ideal* for mixed ability teaching as it provides concepts which can be considered by a variety of age and ability levels.

The loose-leaf format allows teachers to put together any combination of lessons, the cross-referring facilitating the construction of
a complete school course.

Some of the activities recommended by the teachers who used
Language in Use involved working in small groups and using a
"games" approach, which Stott[28] has also suggested as a successful strategy. *Distinctive Voices* was used with fourth year less able
pupils in an inner city school as part of a pilot scheme for a Mode
3 CSE course in Communication Skills. It is based upon a tape
recording which encourages pupils to examine characteristics of
speech and our attitude towards them. In the Field Trial the tape
was played, and pupils identified accent, dialect, articulation,
speed and pitch as features which distinguished voices. Two girls
then taped themselves using "disguised voices" and their classmates were asked to identify the speakers. The group then
discussed the importance of context, and how people modify *what*
they say and *how* they say it in different situations – thus the
pupils showed their awareness of register. The first lesson concluded with an analysis of the voice characteristics of the pupils,
represented in bar graphs, but later lessons included an examination of talk among friends, the family, and a consideration of an
"artificial language – CB speak" when a pupil brought in her
Citizen Band radio to demonstrate.

There are some inherent problems in using *Language in Use* and
even those who were most positive about the materials emphasized the challenge and potential problems because of the underlying assumptions in these materials that teachers

- will accept, with confidence, pupils' needs to develop skills of
  interaction and self-monitoring
- are aware that learning takes place as much through speaking
  and writing as through listening and reading
- are willing to prepare additional materials
- are prepared to be highly selective about choosing material –
  rather than expecting a complete course geared to their
  pupils' needs
- wish to encourage *active* participation.

The Field Report concluded: "Teachers who may teach pupils
with learning difficulties only occasionally, and want them to
accept fairly passive roles would *NOT* welcome this folder."

Professor Alan Blyth and his team have produced *Time, Place
and Society*,[29] which are exceptionally well-planned materials
highly relevant to the hard to teach, despite the high level of

literacy they sometimes require from the reader. In the development of this material, there was a strong emphasis on involving
teachers and incorporating their ideas. An excellent booklet from
the Project deserves to be read and discussed. It draws attention
to twelve "Spotlights". *Spotlight 12* emphasizes the importance of
linking the Project's ideas and materials to the rest of the
curriculum and to the rest of schooling. The team called for the
pursuit of objectives and key concepts and the adjustment of the
programme to particular environments as an alternative to a
chronological syllabus in history or a regional syllabus in
geography; and argued that this would provide a better preparation even for subject-based work. It is an approach that would
seem to have much to offer pupils with learning difficulties and
most teachers who have been introduced to TPS in current field
trials have proved to be enthusiastic about its possibilities. Seven
key concepts were identified at the beginning of the project and
these endured throughout the Project's life. Four of these were
"substantive" and were mainly concerned with processes in
society:

Communication
Power
Values and beliefs
Conflicts/consensus

and three were "methodological" concepts mainly concerned
with ways of analysing society:

Similarity/difference
Continuity/change
Causes and consequences.

Unlike some other humanities projects, TPS tackles only what is
feasible within a normal school. Teachers at a Midlands comprehensive school immediately saw potential lesson material and
possibilities of links with GYSL (Geography for the Young School
Leaver) which was already in use in the school.

   The hard to teach suffer from an increasing sense of literacy
confusion and failure as they move through school. On entry to
secondary school many experience a genuine feeling of handicap
as they try to make sense of both the enormous amount of
reading matter and the new writing demands made upon them.
Nevertheless, then and throughout their school careers, they still
wish to be involved in curriculum activities which they perceive
as normal for secondary school pupils of their age. They resent
being picked out for special lessons and want to participate in the

regular work of their class. Both *Language in Use* and *Time, Place and Society* enable this to occur.

Design and craft education

Design and craft education offers enormous scope for involvement in the community and wider society and it is not uncommon for some of the least likely pupils to show unexpected qualities of co-operation, persistence and initiative. A Schools Council project based at the University of Keele[30] emphasized pupil identification of problems, and design and evaluation of solutions. This Project's materials cover five main areas, shown in Fig. 4.7.

The headmaster of a school where this work was carried out volunteered some reflections on the boys who had so promptly and willingly given their services:

> As I read the names I realized that a number of the boys had appeared before different juvenile courts recently. Two, for instance, had been involved, with others, one evening in smashing a sports shop window and making off with whatever they could grab quickly. They had no use for the articles they took but threw them away. Yet another three had stolen sheath knives during the school holidays, and used them to threaten girls. Serious charges had been made but the boys had claimed it was "just a giggle". Six other boys had been in trouble with the police over fighting at a Fourth Division football match. They also minimized the seriousness of their offence.
>
> It dawned on me with surprise that at least a half of the "Factory Days" volunteers had been involved in acts of hooliganism about the town, and that I had written reports on them for juvenile courts. There was substantial uniformity about the reports. I could not say that any one of them was openly aggressive or unpleasant in school. They were somehow "unorganizable", though forming a clearly distinguishable "sub-group" within their year group. They were the boys who could never bother to bring swimming trunks for baths mornings, or PE kit for games days.

This concept of the "factory day" linked to a community project seemed imaginative and to be offering a real opportunity to break through the crust of indifference and rejection that so many young school leavers have developed:

> The "Factory Days" cut right through the normal timetable, and the disruption made the whole school, particularly young staff, aware of the project. It caught the imagination of those boys most closely involved, and took them on a spiritual adventure such as comes infrequently to us in our lifetime. It was not something pushed to produce house points, but was, as the boys said, "dead

Figure 4.7 Areas covered by art and design project

1. Materials, discovery and design. The development of the design process, upon which this section is based, is fundamental to the Project's thinking. Thus, given a problem, such as the need of some disabled people for a simple piece of equipment that will enable them to perform a particular action, students are encouraged to identify and specify the problem (e.g. what the equipment is for, what materials are advisable), accept the restraints, engage in pre-design and research discussion with other students and teachers, produce models in card, clay, etc., consolidate workable solutions into controlled areas of manufacture, discuss and modify, produce a solution and finally assess its success.

2. Materials and domestic life. Here the pupil is working not only with wood, but with a whole range of materials from plastics to new decorating materials. Work undertaken may include conversion, renovation and maintenance of the home, interior and exterior decoration, layout of gardens, minor building projects and appreciation of household equipment. The whole field of consumer expertise is an integral part of this work and again a problem-solving approach is adopted.

3. Materials and community development. Pupils are encouraged to identify school and community needs, translate these into design terms, formulate proposals and implement these under staff guidance. Projects undertaken in the trial schools included working with geriatric patients, preparing play equipment in educational priority areas and helping to restore parts of Fountains Abbey.

4. Materials and work. In association with colleges of further education, attempts were made to explore the implications of link courses. Production-line situations in the school workshop were developed for short-term adoption to include concepts such as cost–benefit analysis, quantity and variation and labour intensity. Besides school-based "factory day" approaches, the project was also interested in developing schemes of "work experience".

5. Materials and leisure. Included in this section are suggestions for ways in which leisure time can be used, ranging from toy and model making, through photography, karting and land yachts to the theatre.

serious". There was no promise of reward. This project was offered as a yoke, in the same shape almost as the "blood, toil, tears and sweat" of Garibaldi and Churchill. The young "hooligans" accepted this yoke readily, and found it easy, and naturally borne. Had it been presented in any other way it might have been mistaken for a fetter. And youth today is not inclined to wear chains – other than those it chooses for decoration.

Education for family life

There is evidence that young people in schools would like more courses dealing with aspects of family life. Findings from the National Children's Bureau National Child Development Study[31] show that of the 16,000 sixteen-year-olds questioned, 76 per cent were satisfied with the information received in school on reproduction, but only a half were satisfied with information on the growth of children, less than one-third on the care of babies and only 40 per cent on the practical problems of family life. More than half the sample wanted to know more about sexual and family life.

A survey of 4,000 school leavers in Scotland found that nearly half of the girls put "child care" or social education at the top of the list of subjects they would like to know more about (Docherty, 1978).[32]

It is argued here that preparation for parenthood should form an important part of the curriculum for *all* pupils. However, the subject matter, being very varied and easily translatable into concrete terms, is particularly suitable to the hard to teach. Topics suggested in the NCB report include child care, child development, parentcraft education, preparation for family life, personal relationships, design for living, homemaking, sex education, citizenship, family life education, health education. The report noted that preparation for parenthood had seldom been considered an integral part of the curriculum. The aims, objectives and titles of relevant courses presented over the last decade have usually reflected their origins in health education, sex education (often part of the science curriculum), home economics, social education, religious education or pastoral care.

However, efforts have been made to prepare curriculum guidelines[33,34] and to achieve some coherence. In courses of this kind, there does seem to have been a shift away from the more practical aspects such as bathing babies, towards a fuller consideration of the emotional and psychological needs of children; CSE examinations now devote perhaps 30 to 70 per cent of the marks to practical work – working with and observing children. Furthermore, teaching is no longer focused round an idealized nuclear family; a number of syllabuses now include single parenthood and handicap.

The aims and content of an Inner London Education Authority's course 'Child Development and the Family' may be quoted as an example. It aims:

1. To provide for the pupils a course in which, by studying family life and the pre-school child, they themselves may be helped to grow towards maturity and become responsible parents.
2. To encourage a greater awareness of the needs of young children through learning about the environmental and other circumstances which may affect their development.

Schools wishing to create more cohesive courses round themes connected with family education have, thus, the widest possible scope. The best source currently available seems to be the admirably concise *A Job for Life Education and Support for Parents*, again from the National Children's Bureau (1982). It deals with the whole life cycle, from birth to old age, considering for each age group the aims and sources of support, and the needs of the individual. It uses the same strategy to deal with selected themes: "during a committed relationship", "during pregnancy", "as a parent with young children", "as a parent of older children", "as grandparents and parents". It will be useful to the present discussion to quote the section on 11–18 years. (Figure 4.8)

It is not enough merely to arrange "courses"; family education must take for granted a willingness to become involved, to some extent, in the actualities of family life, and it is essential to involve people and agencies outside the school: social workers, health visitors, educational welfare officers, the child guidance clinic, the school nurse and doctor, parents (of course) and voluntary organizations. One of the most sympathetic of the latter are the Family Service Units, which have published a discussion paper *Schools and Families and Social Workers* (1982)[35] offering advice to schools about dealing with parents. It gives, for example, case histories of what goes well and what can go wrong when complex organizations come into contact with often over-wrought parents.

An optimistic note

This chapter began by quoting from Wilf Brennan's demonstration of the inadequacy of secondary programmes for special

Figure 4.8 Aims, needs and sources of support for 11–18-year-olds

Aims of support	To inform, offer appropriate experiences and discussion opportunities in order that children can make balanced decisions about their own lives. To offer individual counselling opportunities at all stages.
Needs of an individual in relation to the development of future parenting skills	To build on previous stages, plus: To adjust to puberty and to own sexuality including responsibilities connected with sexual activity and a comprehensive and practical knowledge of contraception for boys and girls. A widening range of social skills and competence. Ability to relate to peer group and to parents. Emotional maturity and independence. Developing self-knowledge and self-esteem. Developing values and norms of behaviour. Opportunities to achieve intellectual potential. An increasing awareness of adolescent and adult needs and development. An increasing understanding of what is involved in parenting. Opportunities to be with young children. To consider the relationship between work and family. Ability to use leisure time, unemployment and enforced leisure competently.
Sources of support 11–18 years Sources of support	Parents or substitute parents. Family, friends, neighbours and peer group. In school: by teachers and by many others working with them: school counsellors, school health and psychological services, careers officers, education welfare officers and ancillary staff. Through a coherent programme of education for personal relationships and family life. Out of school: by youth and community workers, family planning doctors, young people's advisory services, church workers, etc. Through group work and/or individual counselling.

educational needs, but continued by quoting Jean Roberts talking about enjoyment and widening horizons. Examples of imaginative, excellent, innovatory, attention-commanding materials and teaching have been cited from many areas of the curriculum. The question that has to be answered is why such materials and techniques are not more widely known and used. Why does the teaching of pupils with learning difficulties continue to be so dismal, so dismissive, so inadequate, when it is so easy for satisfactory alternatives to be arranged?

In addition to the few examples in this chapter, I could have given hundreds more instances of successful teaching and, indeed, some years ago I brought together a book[36] of such examples. One of the outstanding experiments described was called "school without walls". Students at Manchester Polytechnic (initial B.Ed. and in-service teachers) combined to work with fifth year pupils from an inner city comprehensive school. One afternoon a week was given over to exploring the resources of the city. Being in pairs with these "tough" youngsters was an educational experience for the student teachers! They went to some unusual places. Mary and George (students) took Franklyn and Arthur (pupils: two extremely withdrawn boys, who had expressed some interest in cars) to a car showroom. They had two aims in mind. First, to explore the pattern of jobs – manager, mechanics, salesmen etc. and how they worked together as a team to produce the business. Second, to encourage the boys to ask some questions for themselves. They recorded their account of the visit and interviews, and the boys were very excited by the tapes because they had not heard their own voices before.

> One anecdote worth mentioning is that during the survey . . . a discussion arose as to why some cars had no year-letter at all. When an "old banger" came round the corner at that moment, the boys and the students jumped up and down in excitement, pointing at the number plate. The car travelled a further hundred yards and the driver got out to examine the machine, convinced it was about to blow up, at least. This incident did a great deal to make the relationship more relaxed. . . . Once again the session finished on an optimistic note: the students left the pupils at 4 p.m. still working on their graphs despite the fact that the bell had gone (perhaps even oblivious of the fact?) . . .

References

1. BRENNAN, W. (1979) *Curricular Needs of Slow Learners*. Schools Council Working Paper 63.
2. GULLIFORD, R. and WIDLAKE, P. (1975) *Teaching Materials for Disadvantaged Pupils*, Schools Council Curriculum Bulletin 5.
3. Bretton Wood Community School (1982) *In Network*, Community Education Development Centre.
4. BRAY, E. (1982) a. "The Clydebank EEC project"; "Work experience", *J. Comm. Ed.* 1,3. b. Materials from this Project are published by Longman Group.
5. Coventry Education Committee (1982) Work preparation: teachers' book; pupils' log book.
6. MITCHELL, G. (1982) "YOP: a fresh look", *J. Comm. Ed.* 1,3.
7. BINDLEY, P. and PARRY, M. (1982) "Adult education and the unemployed", *Adult Education*, 55,2.
8. FLEMING, D. (1982) "Ready for the real world", *J. Comm. Ed.* 1,3.
9. National Elfrida Rathbone Association (1980) Conference report, *Education*, 11 July 1980.
10. FAIRBAIRN, A. (1972) "Better use of time off" in *Industrial Training International*, March 1972.
11. Youthaid (1980) *Education*, 12 December 1980.
12. York conference, Centre for the Study of Comprehensive Schools, *Education*, 31 July 1981.
13. TUNGATT, M.F. and TOWNSEND, A.R. (1980) "Experience of physical education and its influence on later sports activity: a study in North-east England", *Durham and Newcastle Research Review* Vol. IX, No. 44, Spring 1980.
14. PEARSON, J.M. (1977) "Non-participation in games: a specific study". *Br. J. Physical Ed.* 8,6, 1977.
15. WHATLEY, L. and ARMITAGE, J. (1983) Report on *Unemployed Young Women Project*, Community Education Develop. Centre.
16. HOPSON, B. and HOUGH, P. (1973) in MacBEATH, J. and others (1981) *Social Education. Notes Towards a Definition*, Scottish Social Education Project.
17. GUNTER, B. (1982) "Does television interfere with reading development?", *Bulletin of British Psychological Society*, Vol. 35 (June). "Can television teach kindness?", *Bulletin of British Psychological Society*, Vol. 34 (April).
18. PARFIT, C. (1977) "Film in remedial education", *Remedial Education*, 11,2.
19. Notting Dale Urban Studies Centre, *Annual report*.
20. WIDLAKE, P. (1983) "Survey of Schools Council projects for pupils with special educational needs." In Press.
21. *Open Science. Science for the less able child*, Hutchinson & Hart-Davis Educational.
22. *Open Science at Work*, Addison-Wesley.

23. *Less Academically Motivated Pupils project*, Association for Science Education.
24. LUMB, D. and BROWN, M. (1981) *Topic Index of Mathematics Books for Less Gifted Children*, Newcastle-upon-Tyne Advisory Service.
25. COCKROFT, Lord (1982) *Mathematics Counts*, HMSO.
26. DENVIR, B. and others (1982) *Low Attainers in Mathematics 5–16 Policies and Practices in Schools*, Methuen.
27. DOUGHTY, P., PEARCE, J. and THORNTON, G. (1971) *Language in Use*, Edward Arnold.
28. STOTT, D. (1982) *Helping the Maladjusted Child*, Open University Press.
29. BLYTH, W.A.L. *Time, Place and Society*, Schools Council.
30. EGGLESTON, J. *Schools Council project. Art and Design.*
31. FOGELMAN, K. (1976) *Britain's Sixteen Year Olds*, National Children's Bureau.
32. DOCHERTY, B. (1978) Scottish Council for Research in Education.
33. National Children's Bureau (1982) *A Job for Life, Education and Support.*
34. PUGH, G. (1980) *Preparation for Parenthood*, National Children's Bureau.
35. Family Service Units (1982) *Schools and Families and Social Workers.*
36. WIDLAKE, P. (1976) *Successful Teaching in the Urban School*, Ward Lock.

CHAPTER 5

Society's Choice

The gravest consequence of compulsory education, according to Margaret Donaldson[1] "is the feeling of inferiority and low personal worth which it involves in the school failures". The key problem, she felt, was how this could be avoided. The present book has provided an indication of how well some schools are managing not to generate such feelings and as W. D. Wall[2] has elegantly written:

> We really have no choice but to back the one horse we have in the race with catastrophe. Only the school is in a position *vis-a-vis* all families and society in general to provide the inspiration, the means and the vehicle for the kind of evolution in human nature which is now clearly necessary – nothing but a positively educative community will serve and the impulse and much of the conceptual and moral effort to build it will have to come from the professionals of education redefining and assuming a new role.

The need for a new role has been argued throughout the present book. In this final chapter I will draw out some of the implications more clearly, and take up a few points which were touched upon in Chapter 2.

A new role must be based upon a keen awareness of certain changes occurring in our society. Some of the adaptations I have suggested in earlier chapters, particularly in teachers' attitudes, might be regarded as utopian; but I would suggest that, on the contrary, the utopian view is to suppose that state schools can continue to operate as self-contained institutions with curricula organized around examinations which have relevance for only a small minority. A new role must take into account: unemployment, family life and increased tension; and teachers must be prepared to change their working practices, and to learn new knowledge and new skills.

Unemployment

First, it is as well to remind ourselves of the scale, intensity and persistence of unemployment in Britain. An excellent, non-polemical fact-packed book by Giles Merritt[3] sets the scene not just nationally but world wide. Even the official figures (which tend to utilize every device to minimize the total) have admitted well over three million unemployed in 1982 in the United Kingdom; at the time of writing, over one million have been continuously unemployed for a year.

According to Merritt, there is an unpublished OECD report which shows an unemployment graph for the twenty-four richest countries of the world, moving gently from 16.5 million out of work in 1975 to 21 million in 1980 and taking off steeply to 28.5 million in 1982, soaring to 35 million by 1985. Merritt's review of various past estimates of future unemployment indicated that they were nearly always too optimistic, though they were invariably denounced as alarmist by the government of the day when they first appeared. Moreover, these figures exclude the "discouragement" factor – those so put off by the impossibility of finding any employment that they never enter the competition at all, which may add as much as 20–30 per cent.

It does not appear that the vanished manufacturing jobs will ever be recovered – at least this is Merritt's conclusion: "It was the speed and ferocity with which the depression gnawed at the hard industrial core of the manufacturing base that began to provoke the greatest concern, for many of those job losses implied an irreversible contraction of the country's industrial muscle." Summing it all up, including the still unpredictable impact of what he calls the "micro-electronics monster", he rejects the view of the jobs crisis as an avalanche which will soon stop and from which Western economies will soon be able to dig themselves out. "A more realistic analysis," he suggests, "is that of a glacier, which beneath its surface is gouging away at our familiar economic, social and political structures, just as savagely as the glaciers which once landscaped the earth."

The changes may be structural and irreversible; this is a fearfully difficult message to accept. This unwonted and unwanted leisure, which has been predicted for the future, may already have arrived. The gap between prediction and fulfilment of the prophecy reduces almost to vanishing point and nobody can begin to suggest what impact the microchip will have as it becomes more widely used and as new uses are invented. The only certain thing is that it will happen quickly.

The effect on individual lives can be devastating. Unemployment is closely associated with ill-health, deep distress, child cruelty; its effects move on into the next generation. Under 25s are disproportionately represented and in some districts two out of three school leavers were unable to find work in 1981, e.g. Redditch New Town in the Midlands had 74 per cent school leavers unable to find work; Preston, in the North West, had 66 per cent. By the mid-80s (before the microchip begins to bite really hard), "unemployment will have become one of the most widely shared conditions outside of the usual human experiences such as birth, hunger, sex, death".

Of course, Merritt's analysis may not be any more accurate than those he criticizes but it is not possible for any government to do nothing. The options are in fact many, once it is accepted that unemployment is itself extremely costly and that the money might just as well be spent on measures to help people help themselves. This in fact is being done on a grand scale through the Manpower Services Commission and one of the strategies being considered is further education and training. Pupils in schools are, of course, vividly aware of the facts of life about unemployment. There are curricular implications of many kinds, which were drawn out in Chapter 4. Schools will have to take the responsibility for explaining about the disappearance of work and begin to pioneer alternative forms of occupying time. They can take the lead in producing a new attitude.

Changing family structure

The "family" in Britain today is still, in the popular conception, in the view presented by the media and through advertising, and in the implicit assumptions of governments framing policy, a married couple with children. But the true picture is rather different, and has changed quite considerably over the last twenty years. It is now possible to describe a variety of child-rearing situations; single parent families, dual rather than single worker families, large families, reconstituted families (involving step-parents, step-brothers and sisters), families with adopted or fostered parents and extended families. "Thus our assumptions about the nature and quality of family life diverge from the reality for a substantial number of families."

Even so, "the normal pattern of family life *over time* is to grow up in a two parent household with siblings, marry, have children, and have your marriage ended by death rather than divorce".[4] The proportion of marriages ended by divorce has, however, increased 400 per cent since 1971 when the Divorce Law Reform Act was enacted; the rate has doubled for those above 25 and tripled for those below. It is probable that 1 in 4 marriages will now end in divorce, 1 in 3 for those who marry before they are twenty and for those living in inner London. The proportion of one-parent families has also increased so that 1 in 8 of all families are in this category, involving nearly one million children.

It does not follow that children from these different styles of family will necessarily be disturbed or present learning difficulties; but many will, and an increasing number will experience short or long periods in care. Children are often treated as incidents in the life style of parents who are themselves very ill-prepared for the transition to parenthood and for the various adult relationships which accompany the coming of children.

Generalizations about child-rearing behaviours, especially those associated with social class, quickly tend to become *explanations* and, as previously stated, self-fulfilling prophecies. Rather than wasting time trying to identify particular groups as the source of disturbed children, I prefer the approach of an OECD working party which demonstrated how "the emotional functions in the family operate as the source of the unique power of its educational process".[5] Children must be helped to cope with the considerable mental discomfort which is required to learn from experience or they "eject painful feelings outward from the person, leaving him mentally emptied and impoverished". Examples of these two opposite kinds of emotional functions are provided in readily understood terms:

generating love	promoting hate
promoting hope	sowing despair
absorbing depressive feelings	emanating persecutory feelings
thinking	creating lies and confusion

The right hand list denotes forms of relationships in families whose emotional content is literally destructive of the thought processes of family members. The argument is that in order for the positive emotional functions to predominate in the family, it must be organized around the stable *psychological* presence of the parent couple.

The actual family arrangements – male/female couple, single parent in its many variants, etc. – are of less significance than the emotional climate which produces a corresponding and predominant mode of learning in the family; the true or optimum mode only develops in the presence of the positive emotional functions. And, of course, "families" which generate such a climate also tend to be those which integrate with the community, especially the schools.

I am suggesting that schools need to be vividly aware of their pupils' family background, but from a rather different point of view than is usually taken, involving a more sensitive appraisal of the psychological health of the child's situation and avoiding altogether stereotyped judgements based on crude categorizations such as "one-parent family".

Increased social tension

There has been no lack of warnings about the likelihood of civic disorder. As long ago as 1970 Bhattnagar[6] reported on the sense of alienation developing among black adolescents during their schooling and predicted that there would be a backlash. "The time to act is overdue," he wrote twelve years before the outbursts in Bristol, Liverpool, Manchester and London.

Even so, in the words of Lord Scarman's carefully balanced and dignified report on the disorders

> . . . The British people watched with horror and incredulity an instant audio-visual presentation on their television sets of scenes of violence and disorder in their capital city, the like of which had not previously been seen in this century in Britain. In the centre of Brixton, a few hundred young people – most, but not all of them, black – attacked the police on the streets with stones, bricks, iron bars, and petrol bombs, demonstrating to millions of their fellow citizens the fragile basis of the Queen's peace. (para. 1.2)

It would be difficult to improve upon Lord Scarman's analysis of the cause of the disorders.

> Two views have been forcibly expressed in the course of the enquiry as to the causation of the disorders. First is: oppressive policing over a period of years, and in particular, the harassment of young blacks on the streets of Brixton. On this view it is said to be unnecessary to look more deeply for an explanation of the disorders. They were "anti-police". The second is that the disorders, like so many riots in British history, were a protest against society by people, deeply frustrated and deprived, who saw in a violent

attack upon the forces of law and order their one opportunity of
compelling public attention to their grievances. I have no doubt
that each view, even if correct, would be an over-simplification of a
complex situation. If either view should be true, it would not be the
whole truth.[7]

The Scarman report, in the best legal tradition, resolutely
refuses the over-simplification; it balances the social facts against
the evidence on individual conduct; it even-handly attributes
blame to the police, television reports, the legal framework. It
calls for urgent action: a better concerted attack on the problems
of the inner city; more help for ethnic minorities; full community
involvement, not just by minority groups, and especially by the
police; a greater sense of responsibility on the part of the press
and television. There is little evidence that this call for action has
been taken very seriously by the government, but still, the
recommendations were made and that is something.

The conclusion was that the disorders were communal distur-
bances arising from a complex political, social and economic
situation, not special to Brixton. There was a strong racial element
in the disorders but they were not race riots.

It is not difficult to relate these events to school behaviour.
Already, as in Toxteth, Liverpool, there have been direct repur-
cussions. The belief that white teachers are prejudiced against
them is widely held by black pupils and frequently cited as the
main cause of their learning difficulties. One effect of the Scarman
report, in conjunction with the Rampton/Swann Committee,
must surely be to place multicultural education at the top of the
list of priorities, and not only for schools with a high proportion
of pupils from ethnic minority groups. The Scarman report is an
invitation to accept the fact that Britain is now a multicultural
society, for all citizens to inform themselves accordingly and to
examine the extent of their own prejudices. It was small personal
satisfaction to the present writer to have published an article
calling for just such a policy immediately before the riots. The
present book says it again: we must look for ways and means of
enabling our schools to respond more positively to these extreme
demands. There *are* schools and educational systems which are
adopting positive multi-cultural policies and curricula but the
majority of teachers are not convinced that it is necessary unless
they work in schools with a high proportion of ethnic minority
pupils (Bloom and Widlake).[8] Parents' wishes have to be heard
and taken into account in deciding the curriculum. These can be
contradictory, and gratifying one group may increase tension
among another. For example, parents practising the Muslim

religion have strong views about segregation of the sexes, sex education, female roles, food, as well as about the presentation of religious beliefs. Other parents may hold equally strong but contrary views. Nor must the pupils' own views be overlooked. Many parents are deeply dissatisfied with the performance of schools and either wish to withdraw their offspring altogether (as Muslim parents are trying to do in Bradford, by buying some of the schools) or by providing supplementary schooling (such as the Saturday schools organized by West Indian groups). The best efforts of the teaching profession are not always appreciated by those it purports to serve, so it makes absolute sense to try to find out what it is that the parents and pupils are hoping to obtain from schooling.

Changing work patterns for teachers

Some forward-looking Local Education Authorities have given a lead by publishing plans for reorganization which attempt to define the needs of pupils over the next two decades and to take account of them in a revised curriculum. And as the Warnock report has firmly reminded us

> The purpose of education for all children is the same, the goals are the same. But the help that individual children need in progressing towards them will be different.

If a long perspective is taken and the needs of pupils are given priority, many aspects of educational provision, at present often regarded as immutable, come to be seen as problematic. For example, in terms of *delivery of services*, there are serious disadvantages in the fixed terms, holiday arrangements and hours worked by teachers; all these will certainly have to become more flexible, whatever the administrative difficulties. Nor would there seem to be any likelihood of a continuance of a highly structured system of separate institutions, operating on a hierarchy of levels. Co-operation between institutions would seem to be a simple matter, but, in fact, it is only recently that schools and colleges of further education have taken it for granted that facilities will be shared whenever possible. Teachers given responsibility for these arrangements require new skills.

So, too, do teachers who come regularly into contact with parents, volunteers and other adults, professionals or para-professionals. They have received little, if any, training for such work during their college or university courses, and not very much is available on an in-service basis. Perhaps the major change that should be effected in schools is in relation to staff support.

Tim Brighouse, Chief Education Officer for Oxfordshire, suggests that the necessary changes in teacher work patterns are beginning to emerge:

> I am delighted to work in an authority where the overwhelming majority of our teachers have decided to teach in mixed age groups in primary schools. . . . Such schools are mature and civilised, never more so where they have teenagers and parents in them too. We need to take the plunge at the secondary stage . . .[9]

However, he does not mention parallel arrangements for staff training. If schools are to reorganize to meet the needs of the hard to teach, the first element to be settled in planning changes should be staff training. Arrangements for assisting young teachers, in particular, should be carefully considered.

New knowledge and new skills

Numerous cases have been quoted which reveal the extreme abhorrence many pupils have of special treatment. This is especially apparent during adolescence and, if ignored, may produce a reaction so strong as to vitiate the effects of the treatment. For this and other reasons many specialists in learning difficulties have begun to work in regular classrooms, either directly with pupils or in support of other teachers.

It is a useful exercise to draw up a personal checklist of some of the skills and knowledge which specialist teachers might try to acquire in order to be successful in these roles.

1.0 *Communicative competence with colleagues*
   1.1 Skills in preparing, stating and sustaining a case for curriculum change to colleagues both orally and in written form.
   1.2 Skills in personal communication with colleagues and other adults and also in committees or larger group meetings.
   1.3 Knowledge of learning theories covering a wide age range and certainly including something about adults' learning.
   1.4 Knowledge of voluntary and statutory agencies likely to be useful to the school.
2.0 *Communicative competence with pupils*
   2.1 Skills in listening to the pupils' voices (excellent starting

points, in published form, being the consumers' views of British education in *Tales out of School*).[10]

2.2 Skills in achieving empathy with troubled pupils whilst sustaining conditions for learning (David Lane *The Impossible Child*).[11]

2.3 Knowledge of the psychology of the hard to teach and of their cultural milieu . . . . . . (*The Social World of the Comprehensive School* by Glen Turner, gives many instances of school subcultures and pupils' adaptations to them).[12]

2.4 Knowledge of the particular requirements of girls in secondary and further education.

3.0 *Language across the curriculum*

3.1 Knowledge of the language requirements and responsibilities of the subject areas e.g.

Vocabulary: use of technical terms; whether demands made on pupils are excessive.

Special uses of language: use of more complex sentences than usual; use of a very compact, objective language (much use of the passive voice) as in mathematics and science; or of sequence, cause and effect; comparisons of evidence/bias, as in the social sciences (see Marland pp. 74/77, 104/112).[13,14]

3.2 Knowledge of the skills required by pupils e.g.

skills required in using written source material (index, table of contents, skimming and scanning etc.).

Study skills (e.g. note taking; project instructions).

3.3 Teacher's skills e.g.

Using narrative

Giving instructions

Exposition of content

Planning and providing opportunities for talk

Carrying out readability surveys of texts, worksheets and other printed materials, and adapting texts in accordance with linguistic criteria.

4.0 *Learning difficulties across the curriculum*

4.1 Knowledge of the acquisitions of basic skills and of the full range of available materials and approaches to prevention and remediation.

4.2 Knowledge of the linguistic demands in different subject areas; skills in advising specialists on how to adapt; skills in demonstrating techniques.

4.3 Knowledge of the motivational qualities of curriculum materials appropriate to the 14–18 age group; skills in demonstrating their use.

4.4   Psychological knowledge of 14–18 age group; skills in practice.

5.0   *Teaching for transfer*

To develop the pupils' capacity to use newly-acquired skills independently of the situation in which they were learned is the ultimate aim of all teaching. Several examples have been given of ambitious attempts to achieve transfer of learning (for example, McPhail's Moral Education programme). These have frequently started with an analysis of the task to be completed, breaking it down into particular skills to be acquired. Although I have many reservations about the skills model, it does have the considerable merit of forcing us to think about the content of the curriculum in a more realistic framework. A valuable tool for this purpose has been provided by the Further Education Curriculum Review and Development Unit,[15] which attempts to identify the particular skills required in different occupations. For example, mathematical skills and "communication" skills are analysed as in Figures 5.1 and 5.2.

Specialist teachers, it seems to me, now have an excellent opportunity to demonstrate "how to reach the hard to teach" by acquiring knowledge and skills in teaching for transfer. In addition to what is set out below, they need to have instinctively, or to acquire consciously, the knack of achieving empathy with these demanding pupils – to put the art of teaching at the service of the science of learning.

5.1   Knowledge of particular occupations and skills in developing pupil task analyses.
5.2   Knowledge of unemployment procedures and skills in developing pupil task analyses.
5.3   Knowledge of leisure pursuits and skills in developing pupil task analyses.
5.4   Skills in practical teaching and in developing learning materials within these analyses.
5.5   Skills in the evaluation of teaching techniques and learning materials.

The specialist teacher, armed with some such preliminary analysis of job requirements, can make detailed recommendations about the teaching of particular skills as was described in Chapter 4. The extension of such analyses to the world of no work and leisure has not, so far, been properly undertaken. It is a daunting task but one which will eventually have to be undertaken with whatever conviction we can muster.

Preparation for life

The above taxonomy of knowledge and skills presupposes that pupils are being "prepared for life", and that it is society's choice that *all* its young people should be so prepared – not just a select few. Lest this assumption should seem too high minded, I should like to finish this consideration of possible new roles for teachers with a reminder that ideals, though seemingly out of fashion, are by no means irrelevant: certainly not to the health of a state education system, certainly not to those whose work is mainly with the hard to teach.

The Council of Europe, in conjunction with the Department of Education and Science, recently held a conference to present the findings of a three-year project entitled *Preparation for Life*. This project has produced a vast array of publications[16] including a *Declaration* which was adopted at the end-of-Project conference in Strasbourg, May, 1982 – a short, intense document, well worth reading in its entirety. Recommendations from the *Declaration* which are of particular interest are that, with due respect to the educational priorities of member States, and to regional, social, economic, cultural and individual diversity;

A. Education systems should give all young people the opportunity to acquire knowledge, skills and attitudes in the following key areas, which are closely interdependent:

(i) Life in a democratic society. This should include Human Rights and fundamental freedoms, and duties and responsibilities of citizens, and politics and economics;

(ii) Personal life. This should include: fundamental values, personal and family relations, and personal decision-making;

(iii) Working life. In the compulsory school, preparation for working life should strengthen young people's knowledge of technology. Careers education should be concerned with a broad perspective on working life. In technical and vocational studies, specialization should be carried out gradually after training in the elements which are common to the field in question. All young people are entitled to vocational training;

(iv) Cultural life. This should include an introduction to the cultural, spiritual, historical and scientific heritage, and preparation for life in a multicultural society.

Figure 5.1 Mathematical skills

Skill Descriptors	Clerical	Selling	Professional	Service	Textiles and Clothing	Skilled Engineering	Construction/Building
Use whole numbers	★	★	★	★	★	★	★
Add or subtract whole numbers	★	★	★	★	●	●	○
Use of length – imperial	○	●	●		●	★	★
Estimate	○	●	●	●	○	○	○
Use decimals	★	★	★	○		○	
Use fractions	○	○	○			●	●
Use of length – metric	○		○		○	★	●
Read charts	○	○	●	○		●	
Measure length – metric				○		●	○
Add or subtract decimals	●	★	★	○			
Fill in a time sheet						○	○
Use weight – imperial			●	○	○		
Sums with time				○			○
24-hour clock				○		○	○
Use percentages	●	●	●				
Multiply and divide whole numbers – simple							

Source: *Basic Skills*, F.E.U.[15]

B. There should be a partnership between the school and other social institutions. In particular, the following should interact with the school:

   (i)   The family, through close co-operation with parents;

   (ii) The local community, through: community involvement in the life of the school; voluntary social service by young people; and environmental improvement projects;

   (iii) Political and social institutions, through discussions with leaders of public opinion, political parties, and interest groups; the study of, and visits to, local and national

Figure 5.2 Communication and interpersonal skills

Skill Descriptors	Clerical	Selling	Professional	Service	Textiles and Clothing	Skilled Engineering	Construction/Building	Packing and Assembly
Receive written information	★	●	★	○		●	○	○
Advise or help colleagues or workmates	○	○	★	●	○	★	●	○
Complete standard forms or letters	★	●	★	○	○	○	○	●
Use codes	★	★	●	○	●	○	○	●
Write notes, letters, memos, short reports	★	●	★	★			○	○
File or sort things	★	●	★	○		○		○
Fill in a record book or manual	●		★	●		○	○	○
Look up written information	★	●	●	○			○	
Advise or help customers or clients	○	★	★	●				
Receive complaints	○	●	○	○				
Negotiate with colleagues or workmates	○	○	○	○				

Source: *Basic Skills*, F.E.U.[15]

Key to Figs. 5.1, 5.2
★ Very important skills
● Important skills
○ Less important skills
  Unimportant skills

public institutions; and appropriate out-of-school activities;

(iv) Other countries, through wide-ranging personal contacts, exchanges and school twinning and correspondence. This will involve the knowledge of foreign languages;

   (v) The world of work, through work experience and contacts with representatives of employers and of trade unions;

  (vi) The world of culture in the widest sense, through active participation in social, sports and cultural clubs as well as through contacts with experts and visits to museums, art galleries, concerts, the theatre, the cinema, laboratories, and mass media centres.

C. Pupils should be encouraged to involve themselves actively and increasingly in their preparation for life, by being given opportunities:

   (i) To participate in informed decision-making and to engage in dialogue and negotiation with those responsible for their education;

  (ii) To assume responsibilities towards themselves, their classmates, their school, their family, their peer-groups and their community;

 (iii) To practise forms of delegation and representation;

 (iv) To join school councils and informal students' groups.

Conclusion

The challenges from within and without are such that no school can continue to teach its present curriculum in an unchanged form. The new conditions apply *particularly* to pupils with special educational needs; any regime which concentrates on their difficulties and ignores their reactions to the turmoil around them is unlikely to be effective, even if feasible.

Schools, being so heavily involved in certification, are bound to experience problems in devising programmes for pupils with special needs. The increasing disenchantment of some of these pupils provides an unanswerable case for fresh approaches. Accounts have been given of schools which are conducting experiments of various kinds in both organizational forms and curriculum. The starting point for successful innovation, it is suggested, should be a study of the processes of change in terms of the people involved; the teacher, the parents, the administrative team, the *pupils*. A great deal could be learned if the latter group really had a hearing. Pupils like Victor (one of many interviewed by Daphne Johnson and her colleagues in their study of *Disaffected Pupils*)[17] often find the school curriculum boring and irrelevant but are not necessarily narrow or restricted in their interests. Out of school, Victor had a spare time job in a local club;

he pursued his hobby of aircraft spotting with energy and thoroughness, travelling to airshows whenever possible and devising labour-saving filing systems for the data to be accumulated. "Efficient and opportunist (his) standards are essentially self-devised."

We ought to become more accustomed to the idea of paying attention to the views of the individual within the schools; we ought to make every effort to involve the school with the community it serves, with other branches of the formal education service, with the opportunities being provided by the Manpower Services Commission, with every organization concerned with the creation of informal educational opportunities. The image of the educative community badly requires refurbishment: learning is a lifelong activity of which schooling is but a part and the more eagerly this notion is accepted by schools, the more likely it is that schools will retain some appeal for pupils like Victor who, amazing though it may seem to the sceptical, really do have "standards" about the activities they care about.

What we can try for has been admirably expressed by Smedley:

> Teaching in schools where aggression and boredom were often keynotes, it quickly became evident that *attempted* understanding was the most that human frailty and isolation could manage. Yet this was something. Even "tough" pupils, it was found, tended to respond to an effort to empathise with their attitudes to work and life.

Such efforts should certainly not be confused with "softness" or sentimentality. It is a well-attested pedagogic principle that if you treat people as they are, they will stay as they are. But if you treat them as if they were what they ought to be, they might become what they could be.

References

1. DONALDSON, Margaret (1980) in *All the time in the world Education in a changing society*, Scottish Education Department.
2. WALL, W.D. as reference 1.
3. MERRITT, G. (1981) *World out of work*, Collins.
4. Study Commission on the Family (1980) *Happy Families? A Discussion Paper on Families in Britain*, 3 Park Road, London NW1.
5. OECD Centre for Educational Research and Innovation (1980) *The Educational Role of the Family*, Unpublished.

6. BHATTNAGAR, J. (1970) *Immigrants at School*, Cornmarket Press.
 7. LORD SCARMAN (1981) *The Brixton Disorders: 10–12 April 1981 Report of an Enquiry*, London, HMSO.
 8. BLOOM, D. and WIDLAKE, P. (1979) "Assimilation versus Cultural Pluralism" *Education*, 1 December 1979.
 9. BRIGHOUSE, T. (1983) Paper given at Community Education Association Conference, Birmingham.
10. WHITE, R. and BROCKINGTON, D. (1983) *Tales out of School. Consumers' views of British Education*, Routledge & Kegan Paul.
11. LANE, D. (1978) *The Impossible Child*, Inner London Education Authority.
12. TURNER, G. (1983) *The Social World of the Comprehensive School*, Croom Helm.
13. MARLAND, M. (1977) *Language Across the Curriculum*, Heinemann.
14. HINSON, M. and HUGHES, M. (1982) *Planning Effective Progress*, Hulton/Nare.
15. Further Education Curriculum Review and Development Unit (1982) *Basic Skills Dept. of Education & Science*.
16. Council of Europe (1982) The Council for Cultural Co-operation's Project No. 1: "Preparation for Life", Strasbourg.
17. JOHNSON, D. *et al.* (1982) *Disaffected Pupils*, Brunel University.
18. SMEDLEY, B. (1976). "An approach through attempted understanding". *In* Widlake, P. (Ed.) *Successful Teaching in the Urban School*. Ward Lock.

Index

purposes of, 73
see also educational psychologists,
moral education, remedial
education, sex education, social
education, special education,
supplementary education
educational psychologists, 56, 58
"Elaboration of Complaints, The", 58, 59
employment
changes in, 16, 79–80, 81–2
see also unemployment
"enabling skills", 19, 21
ethnic minorities, 114–15
and Disruptive Units, 33
see also Minority Group Support Service

family
change in structure, 16, 111–13
education for family life, 103–4
family problems
case studies, 4–5, 5–6, 6–7, 7–8
Family Service Units
*Schools and Families and Social
Workers*, 104
Field Report, 99
films
making of, 87–9
Freire, Paulo, 15
Fry Graph, 48
Further Education Curriculum Review
and Development Unit, 118, 120, 121

geography
and reading difficulties, 49
and success rate with slow learners, 71
George Stephenson High School, 39

Health Education Council
health topic questionnaire, 41, 43
hearing problems
case study, 8–9
history
and reading difficulties, 49
and success rate with slow learners, 71
home conditions
changing, 16, 111–13
see also family
humanities, 99–103
Humanities Curriculum Project, 44
humour, 22

Indian pupils
case study, 5–6
Industrial Training Research Unit (ITRU)
recordings of conversations based
on assessment forms, 41, 42

integration
of pupils with special needs and rest
of school, 31, 32, 35
within remedial department, 32

*Job for Life, Education and Support for
Parents, A*, 104, 105

Kent Mathematics Project, 92, 94

LAMP(Less Academically Motivated
Pupils) Project, 92
Language in Use, 98–9, 101
Language, Literacy and Numeracy
Support Service, 37–8
"language" training, 97–9
leisure, 16, 17, 82–4, 110–11
and art and design project, 102
life, preparation for, 119–22
local education authorities
and changing society, 115
and microcomputers, 87
and the *Technical and Vocational
Educational Initiative*, 78, 79
assisting community schools, 24, 25
combatting racism, 31
Inner London Education Authority
course, 'Child Development
and the Family', 104
see also Coventry LEA and
Manchester Education Authority

Making the change, 19, 20
Manchester Education Authority
creation of Language, Literacy and
Numeracy Support Service, 37–8
Manpower Services Commission
and unemployment, 111
*Technical and Vocational
Educational Initiative*, 78–9
mathematics, 92–4
Mathematics for the Majority, 92, 94
microtechnology
effects of, 111
learning about, 89–90
Midlands Mathematics Experiment, 94
Mini Co-operative Companies, 73–6
Minimal Phonic Cues (MPC), 62–5
Minority Group Support Service, 30
moral education, 94–7
Moral Education Curriculum Project,
45, 94–7
Morris, Henry, 24

National Children's Bureau
*Job for Life, Education and Support for
Parents, A*, 104, 105
National Child Development Study, 103

Index